CIVIL RIGHTS

CIVIL RIGHTS

GREAT
SPEECHES
IN
HISTORY

Jill Karson,
Book Editor

Daniel Leone, *President*

Bonnie Szumski, *Publisher*

Scott Barbour, *Managing Editor*

GREENHAVEN
PRESS®

THOMSON
─────✦─────™
GALE

San Diego • Detroit • New York • San Francisco • Cleveland
New Haven, Conn. • Waterville, Maine • London • Munich

© 2003 by Greenhaven Press. Greenhaven Press is an imprint of The Gale Group, Inc.,
a division of Thomson Learning, Inc.

Greenhaven® and Thomson Learning™ are trademarks used herein under license.

For more information, contact
Greenhaven Press
27500 Drake Rd.
Farmington Hills, MI 48331-3535
Or you can visit our Internet site at http://www.gale.com

Cover credit: © Hulton/Archive by Getty Images
Library of Congress, 34, 39, 60, 67, 79, 125, 131
National Archives, 28, 120

LIBRARY OF CONGRESS CATALOGING-IN-PUBLICATION DATA

Civil rights / Jill Karson, book editor.
    p. cm. — (Greenhaven Press's great speeches in history)
  Includes bibliographical references and index.
  ISBN 0-7377-1594-4 (pbk. : alk. paper) — ISBN 0-7377-1593-6 (lib. : alk. paper)
    1. African Americans—Civil rights—History—20th century—Sources. 2. Civil
rights movements—United States—History—20th century—Sources. 3. United
States—Race relations—Sources. 4. Speeches, addresses, etc., American.
  I. Karson, Jill. II. Great speeches in history series.
  E185.61 .C5913 2003
  323.1'73—dc21   2002032209

Printed in the United States of America

Contents

Chapter 1: Civil Rights Pioneers

   Frederick Douglass
   Blacks are morally and intellectually equal to
   whites; therefore, a nation that celebrates the principles of freedom and liberty on Independence Day—
   while at the same time enslaving millions of black
   Americans—is hypocritical and unjust.

   Booker T. Washington
   Only through education, self-improvement, and in-
   dustriousness can blacks uplift themselves to fully
   participate in American society.

   W.E.B. Du Bois
   Blacks must be granted the same political, civil, and
   social rights that white Americans enjoy. Strong
   black leadership and aggressive action are necessary
   to secure these rights.

   Mary Church Terrell
   Race relations in American society are intolerable.
   Black Americans—including black women and children—are oppressed, persecuted, and deprived of in-
   centives to uplift themselves.

Chapter 2: Goals of the Civil Rights Movement

Foreword

I have a dream that one day this nation will rise up and live out the true meaning of its creed: "We hold these truths to be self-evident: that all men are created equal."

I have a dream that one day on the red hills of Georgia the sons of former slaves and the sons of former slave owners will be able to sit down together at the table of brotherhood.

I have a dream that one day even the state of Mississippi, a state sweltering with the heat of injustice, sweltering with the heat of oppression, will be transformed into an oasis of freedom and justice.

I have a dream that my four little children will one day live in a nation where they will not be judged by the color of their skin but by the content of their character.

Perhaps no speech in American history resonates as deeply as Martin Luther King Jr.'s "I Have a Dream," delivered in 1963 before a rapt audience of 250,000 on the steps of the Lincoln Memorial in Washington, D.C. Decades later, the speech still enthralls those who read or hear it, and stands as a philosophical guidepost for contemporary discourse on racism.

What distinguishes "I Have a Dream" from the hundreds of other speeches given during the civil rights era are King's eloquence, lyricism, and use of vivid metaphors to convey abstract ideas. Moreover, "I Have a Dream" serves not only as a record of history—a testimony to the racism that permeated American society during the 1960s—but it is also a historical event in its own right. King's speech, aired live on national television, marked the first time that the grave injustice of racism was fully articulated to a mass audience in a way that was both logical and evocative. Julian Bond, a fellow participant in the civil rights movement and student of King's, states that

> King's dramatic 1963 "I Have a Dream" speech before the Lincoln Memorial cemented his place as first among equals in civil rights leadership; from this first televised mass meeting, an American audience saw and heard the unedited oratory of America's finest preacher, and for the first time, a mass white audience heard the undeniable justice of black demands.

Moreover, by helping people to understand the justice of the civil rights movement's demands, King's speech helped to transform the nation. In 1964, a year after the speech was delivered, President Lyndon B. Johnson signed the Civil Rights Act, which outlawed segregation in public facilities and discrimination in employment. In 1965, Congress passed the Voting Rights Act, which forbids restrictions, such as literacy tests, that were commonly used in the South to prevent blacks from voting. King's impact on the country's laws illustrates the power of speech to bring about real change.

Greenhaven Press's Great Speeches in History series offers students an opportunity to read and study some of the greatest speeches ever delivered before an audience. Each volume traces a specific historical era, event, or theme through speeches— both famous and lesser known. An introductory essay sets the stage by presenting background and context. Then a collection of speeches follows, grouped in chapters based on chronology or theme. Each selection is preceded by a brief introduction that offers historical context, biographical information about the speaker, and analysis of the speech. A comprehensive index and an annotated table of contents help readers quickly locate material of interest, and a bibliography serves as a launching point for further research. Finally, an appendix of author biographies provides detailed background on each speaker's life and work. Taken together, the volumes in the Greenhaven Great Speeches in History series offer students vibrant illustrations of history and demonstrate the potency of the spoken word. By reading speeches in their historical context, students will be transported back in time and gain a deeper understanding of the issues that confronted people of the past.

Introduction

On February 1, 1960, four freshmen from the Negro Agricultural and Technical College in Greensboro, North Carolina, entered Woolworth's Department Store, and, after purchasing several items, took seats at the whites-only lunch counter. When the waitress refused to serve them, the polite but fiercely resolute foursome remained seated until the store closed.

They returned the next day with twenty black students. News of the "sit-ins" galvanized student support across campus, and by the third day, sixty students had joined the movement. Soon, student groups throughout the South were participating in this pioneering form of social protest. Each group was committed to a single goal and a simple code of conduct: They would dress neatly and behave courteously, but they would remain seated at the lunch counter until they were served. They would look straight ahead, and most importantly, they would not respond to taunts, insults, or abuse—no matter how severe—with violence.

Although at times it proved overwhelmingly difficult to remain calm and peaceful, the students persevered. Civil rights activist John Lewis later described the sometimes violent retaliation to which the students were subjected despite their good behavior:

> A group of young white men came in and began pulling people off the lunch-counter stools, putting lighted cigarettes out in our hair or faces or down our backs, pouring catsup and hot sauce all over us, pushing us to the floor and beating us. . . . They didn't arrest a single person that beat us, but they arrested all of us and charged us with disorderly conduct.

Within weeks, sit-ins, boycotts, and demonstrations forced the integration of restaurants and other public facilities across the South. The victory was stunning, not only because blacks and whites could sit side by side in restaurants and movie theaters but also because it proved that nonviolent protest and mass action could effect social change.

The college students who dared to challenge segregated lunch counters and others like them were part of what is today called the civil rights movement, the quest by African Americans to gain political, social, and economic equality that peaked between the years 1957 and 1965. Although the sit-in campaigns were indeed pivotal in this turbulent era, the struggle for racial equality had been under way long before four young men refused to give up their seats at Woolworth's.

The Legacy of Slavery

The mass migration of blacks to America began in the early 1600s, when English colonists brought slaves in shackles and chains to North America. Subjugated in every way, slaves were subjected to extreme hardships and denied even the most basic freedoms. At the end of the Civil War, more than 4 million slaves were freed from bondage. Although their hard-won freedom imbued them with a great sense of optimism, blacks were not to see racism and inequality vanquished in that time, especially in the South. Between the years 1865 and 1875—the Reconstruction era—many state and national leaders attempted to ease the slaves' transition to freedom and safeguard their rights through the national legislature. For example, the Thirteenth Amendment meant that blacks were no longer official "property"; the Fifteenth Amendment granted black men the right to vote; and the Civil Rights Acts of 1866 and 1875 affirmed, respectively, that blacks are U.S. citizens and that black males have the right to vote.

These constitutional guarantees were, for the most part, in theory only, as blacks did not come close to enjoying full citizenship and racial equality. Racism was particularly vehement in the South, where slavery had predominated for so many years. White Southerners remained determined to thwart black advances and conspired a variety of means to keep blacks completely disfranchised. One of the most harrowing examples was the birth of the Ku Klux Klan (KKK), an organization that openly rallied its members to attain its chief objective: to retain white supremacy at any cost. Perhaps the ultimate blow to civil rights came in 1896, when the Supreme Court—overturning any gains made during Reconstruction—upheld a law that separated railroad passengers by race in the case of *Plessy v. Ferguson*. This ruling, and its "separate-but-equal" principle, gave white society a legal basis for segregation—and a powerful weapon to deny blacks the same rights enjoyed by their white counterparts.

By 1900, Jim Crow laws—enacted by Southern states to keep hotels, restaurants, theaters, rest rooms, and even drinking fountains rigidly segregated—were a deeply entrenched reality. Not only as a result of racist legislation but also as a matter of custom and tradition, Jim Crow kept blacks mired in poverty and bereft of any means to progress socially or economically.

A Changing Outlook

The turn of the century brought a cadre of new leaders ready to launch a full assault against the injustices being inflicted on blacks. In this climate, a handful of activists sought an effective means to harness their political power. In 1909, W.E.B. Du Bois and others founded the National Association for the Advancement of Colored People (NAACP), an organization dedicated to ending segregation and securing civil rights through lobbying, agitation, and legal action. Although reform came slowly, the NAACP relentlessly—and many times successfully—attacked segregation in education, transportation, housing, and public facilities. The group's victories, in turn, spurred more blacks to become politically active, and the campaign for civil rights broadened in the black community.

At the same time, the Industrial Revolution resulted in sophisticated farm equipment that eclipsed black field labor, prompting blacks to travel north in search of jobs. World War I heightened this migration as blacks, eager to work, fled north to take advantage of the burgeoning defense industry. The infusion of blacks, however, aggravated problems, such as a rising postwar unemployment in predominantly white Northern cities.

Although a small but growing number of whites joined the movement to improve conditions for blacks, racial problems prevailed into the 1940s. Then, with America's entry into World War II, came a painful contradiction: Black soldiers fought and died to oppose the racist Nazi regime in Europe and promote freedom abroad. Yet those very ideals for which they had risked their lives were nothing but pretenses at home. Coupled with the redistribution of the black population and surging black aspirations, these developments brought a new sense of urgency to race relations during the mid-twentieth century.

The Birth of a Movement

Two incidents captivated the nation—and catapulted civil rights issues into national prominence. The first spark came when the NAACP won an unprecedented courtroom victory during the early 1950s. For years, the famed lawyer for the NAACP, Thurgood Marshall, had been working to overturn the 1896 *Plessy v. Ferguson* decision that supported segregation. In 1954, Marshall, building on earlier cases, argued *Brown v. Board of Education of Topeka, Kansas,* before the U.S. Supreme Court. On May 17, 1954, the Court ruled that segregation in public schools was illegal. The "separate-but-equal" doctrine established by *Plessy v. Ferguson* was, the High Court decided, not protected by the Constitution.

In presenting the Court's decision, Chief Justice Earl Warren described the damaging effect of racial segregation within the schools:

> Segregation of white and colored children in public schools has a detrimental effect upon the colored children. The impact is greater when it has the sanction of the law; for the policy of separating the races is usually interpreted as denoting the inferiority of the Negro group. A sense of inferiority affects the motivation of a child to learn. Segregation, with the sanction of law, therefore, has a tendency to

inhibit the educational and mental development of Negro children and deprive them of some of the benefits they would receive in a racially integrated school system.

Although *Brown v. Board of Education* officially paved the way for school integration, segregationist policies and traditions did not disappear. Many schools, for example, were slow to comply with the Court's ruling. At the same time, the threat of harassment and even violence kept many blacks from enrolling in predominantly white schools. Meanwhile, the black schools in the South remained run-down, overcrowded, and severely underfunded.

The second major development unfolded in Montgomery, Alabama, where a seamstress named Rosa Parks unwittingly launched a campaign that would create the momentum for the entire civil rights movement. On December 1, 1955, the quiet and unassuming Parks—tired after a day's work—boarded a city bus and made her way to the back rows, where blacks were expected to sit. By custom, too, blacks were to give their seats to white passengers when the front seats were filled. On this evening, however, Parks refused to yield her seat to a white man. Impassive, Parks was arrested.

Leaders of the NAACP saw Parks's arrest as an opportunity to challenge Montgomery's racist bus laws. Almost immediately, black leaders throughout Montgomery rallied behind Parks and the NAACP to demand that the city integrate its buses. They nominated Martin Luther King Jr., a relatively obscure Baptist minister at the time, to organize and lead a citywide bus boycott. Accepting his new position, King stressed his nonviolent approach to civil disobedience, setting a tone that would largely characterize the entire civil rights movement: "There will be no threats and intimidation. . . . Our actions must be guided by the deepest principles of our Christian faith. Love must be our regulating ideal."

Four days after Parks's arrest, the Montgomery bus boycott began—and lasted one long, painful year. Throughout the battle in Montgomery, boycotters endured taunts and harassment—and frequent arrests—yet refused to capitulate. Finally, the federal courts intervened and declared segregation on buses unconstitutional.

The Montgomery bus boycott outcome was important on several counts. First, it marked one more victory over insidious Jim Crow laws. More importantly, it inspired a flood of wide-scale resistance to civil rights abuses throughout the South. The boycott also identified King as a national civil rights leader. Passionate, articulate, and dedicated to nonviolence, he would inspire large-scale participation in the civil rights movement.

By 1957, the crusade for civil rights was well under way. That year, Congress passed the first Civil Rights Act since Reconstruction, which ostensibly strengthened voting rights and also established a civil rights division in the Justice Department. King, too, became highly visible as head of the newly formed Southern Christian Leadership Conference (SCLC), a Christian-based civil rights organization that sought to remove the barriers in society that hindered race relations. Its programs included voter registration drives and direct-action protest. At the same time, the NAACP continued its legal campaigns unabated.

With sit-ins grabbing the media spotlight in 1960, legions of young blacks came forward to work for their cause. They participated in rallies, demonstrations, and boycotts. As expectations swelled, other civil rights organizations rose to prominence. In addition to a number of ad hoc civil rights groups that joined the fray, the Student Nonviolent Coordinating Committee (SNCC) was formed in 1960. Like the SCLC, the group was committed to Christian principles, although it was less patient in its approach to civil rights. Membership burgeoned, too, in the Congress of Racial Equality (CORE), an integrated civil rights organization founded during the 1940s to challenge segregation through peaceful protest. In 1961, CORE garnered massive media attention as it targeted segregation in interstate travel.

Freedom Rides

Although the Supreme Court had banned segregation on buses and in bus terminals and rest areas, change came slowly. Federally mandated integration was largely ignored, and many blacks were too intimidated to exercise their constitu-

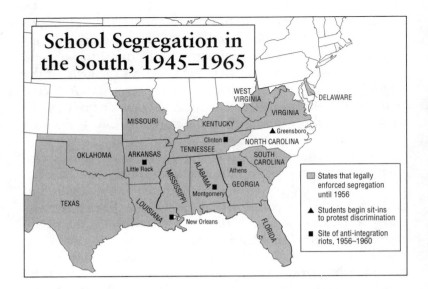

School Segregation in the South, 1945–1965

WEST VIRGINIA

DELAWARE

VIRGINIA

MISSOURI   KENTUCKY

▲ Greensboro

Clinton ■   NORTH CAROLINA

OKLAHOMA   ARKANSAS   TENNESSEE

SOUTH CAROLINA

Little Rock ■

Athens ■

ALABAMA   GEORGIA

MISSISSIPPI   Montgomery ■

TEXAS

LOUISIANA

New Orleans

FLORIDA

☐ States that legally enforced segregation until 1956

▲ Students begin sit-ins to protest discrimination

■ Site of anti-integration riots, 1956–1960

tional rights. In response, CORE organized an interracial band of volunteers to participate in what would become known as Freedom Rides. On May 4, 1961, two commercial buses loaded with Freedom Riders embarked on a road trip through the South to force the integration of buses, terminals, and facilities along the way.

Freedom Riders were met with open hostility: They were taunted, threatened, and attacked on several occasions. In one dangerous incident, a busload of Freedom Riders was besieged by an angry white mob that hurled a firebomb into the bus. As the volunteers fled from the burning vehicle, they were attacked and viciously beaten. Across the nation, people were moved by the Freedom Riders' unwavering adherence to their nonviolent philosophy despite brutal attacks against them.

As the 1960s unfolded, civil rights protests continued to spread across the South. SNCC volunteers bravely sponsored their own Freedom Rides, prompting newly elected president John F. Kennedy to dispatch federal marshals to guarantee their safety. Meanwhile, in Albany, Georgia, local black leaders formed the Albany Movement to push for desegregation and voting rights. The Albany Movement generated great enthusiasm and attracted thousands of protesters from various organizations; however, its lack of a unified front rendered it ineffective.

Although the Albany Movement was somewhat of a debacle, King and other black leaders set their sights on a new stage: Birmingham, Alabama, home of the notoriously racist police chief, Eugene "Bull" Connor. King launched his carefully planned campaign in early 1963. When he was later arrested and jailed, he composed his celebrated "Letter from Birmingham Jail," which garnered for him the support of many whites.

Meanwhile, as the protesters continued their desegregation campaign in Birmingham, an event occurred that captured the nation's attention: Bull Connor—in full view of television cameras—turned water cannons and snarling police dogs on the nonviolent marchers. Mass arrests followed. The news footage not only spurred more blacks into action, but it also fueled outrage and sympathy in the white community. After a month of the highly publicized violence, city officials acquiesced to black demands, and the city's public facilities were desegregated.

Backlash

As the desegregation movement spread, so, too, did fierce resistance in the white community, especially in the Deep South, where a majority of whites subscribed to the myth of white superiority. With blacks chipping away at discrimination in housing, employment, and quality of education, whites devised ever-bolder strategies to sabotage their efforts. These included the formation of white citizen councils, legal battles to outlaw the NAACP, and the general threat of violence.

In one highly publicized incident, Governor Ross Barnett of Mississippi attempted to prevent the admission of James Meredith to the University of Mississippi. Similarly, Alabama's newly elected governor, George Wallace—who had unabashedly promised in his 1963 inaugural address to preserve "segregation forever"—tried to block two black students from enrolling at the University of Alabama. In both cases, federal intervention guaranteed the students' admission. Later the same year, NAACP leader Medgar Evers was ambushed and

shot by a white supremacist. News of Evers's death further ag-
itated the swelling ranks of civil rights activists.

Civil Rights Legislation

In light of such events, it became clear that government intervention was necessary to secure civil rights. To that end,
black leaders from a broad array of civil rights organizations
began plotting a massive campaign to put pressure on the
Kennedy Administration to pass a major federal civil rights
bill. On August 28, 1963, the historic March on Washington
brought approximately 250,000 people to the nation's capital. Although a multitude of memorable speakers addressed
the crowds, the highlight of the event occurred when Martin
Luther King Jr. ascended the platform and delivered his impassioned "I Have a Dream" speech.

The March on Washington generated high hopes as it
pushed Congress toward the passage of the Civil Rights Act,
broad legislation that outlawed discrimination in employment
and in public places, including those that received federal
funds. Although many blacks grew disheartened as the proposal seemed to languish in Congress, Lyndon B. Johnson,
who became president upon Kennedy's assassination in November 1963, finally pushed the legislation through in 1964.

As changes were taking place, SNCC focused its attention on voting rights. To dramatize its cause, the group
launched a series of voter registration drives throughout the
South in 1964, placing particular emphasis on Mississippi,
where less than 5 percent of the state's eligible blacks were
registered to vote. By 1965 the campaign had shifted to
Selma, Alabama. Under King's leadership, thousands of
demonstrators embarked on a fifty-mile walk from Selma to
Montgomery. As the peaceful marchers approached the Ed-
mund Pettus Bridge on March 7, they were blocked by
Selma's sheriff, James Clark, who was not only backed up by
hundreds of state troopers but was also supported by Governor George Wallace. As a horrified nation watched via television, Clark and his officers—wielding nightsticks and even
electric cattle prods—viciously beat the civil rights workers.
Even women and children were attacked.

In response to "Bloody Sunday," thousands of people converged on Selma to join the protesters and support their cause—the protection of voting rights for all Americans. In late March, three thousand people reconvened and completed the march to Montgomery, this time under the protection of the Alabama National Guard. Shortly after, on August 6, 1965, President Johnson signed into law the Voting Rights Act.

Black Militancy

As the 1960s progressed, the civil rights movement began to change. Dismantling Jim Crow laws and expanding voting rights had dominated the late 1950s and early 1960s. By 1965, however, poverty and discrimination in the North—insidious albeit not legislated—had come to the forefront of the civil rights debate.

Although King's nonviolent direct action program had been a popular approach to race problems thus far, many blacks were growing frustrated with the slow progress of civil rights. Even organizations like the NAACP came under attack as blacks moved away from tactics they viewed as hopelessly conservative and outmoded. At the same time, many were skeptical that blacks and whites could live together in a racially integrated society. As a generation of blacks redefined themselves, their changing views heralded the rise of more radical strategies—and more militant leaders.

Malcolm X

As King continued to preach passivity and racial harmony, a new black leader rose to the fore. Intense and articulate, Malcolm X urged complete separation from the white race. In direct opposition to King, Malcolm rejected the notion that nonviolence could counter racial problems. Instead, Malcolm rallied disfranchised young blacks to secure their rights "by any means necessary."

After a pilgrimage to Mecca in 1964, he converted to orthodox Islam. Although he continued to advocate militant black nationalism, he no longer promoted complete separation from whites, believing that cooperation between the races was possible.

Malcolm was assassinated in 1965 while addressing a crowd in New York City. His militant philosophy and separatist ideology, however, were perpetuated by a number of organizations. SNCC, for example, hardened its agenda and began advocating a program of "black power," a term that referred not only to taking pride in black culture but also—among the more militant blacks—the complete separation of the races. CORE, too, renounced some of its long-held beliefs in favor of black power. One extremely provocative black nationalist group to emerge was the Black Panthers, originating in Oakland, California, in 1966. Boldly embracing Malcolm X's mantra "by any means necessary," the Black Panthers brazenly carried weapons as they patrolled their neighborhoods.

In this highly charged atmosphere, riots exploded in Watts, a ghetto section of Los Angeles, California, in 1965. The scope of destruction was staggering: Thirty-four people were killed and—following days of looting and burning—property damages were estimated to exceed $40 million. Watts, though, marked only the first of many outbreaks of black violence. Between 1965 and 1968, similar scenes played out in cities across America, where blacks trapped in urban slums lashed out against the poverty and racism in their communities. The worst uprising occurred in Detroit, Michigan, where forty-three people died during the summer of 1967.

Seen on television, the riots ignited a storm of controversy, deepening the chasm between those who believed that civil rights could only be obtained through violence and those who continued to subscribe to a more peaceful philosophy. At the same time, the lure of black nationalist groups—and radical campaigns—proved irresistible to a broad group of blacks who were no longer willing to wait for slow change.

Responding, in part, to the amplified militancy growing within the movement, King and other black leaders launched a campaign to draw national attention to the most pressing problem plaguing the black community: the lack of economic opportunity. As he began organizing a massive "Poor People's March" to highlight working people's economic plight, King traveled to Memphis, Tennessee, to participate in a garbage workers' strike. On April 4, 1968, King was gunned down as he stood on the balcony of his hotel room.

King's death was a crippling blow to the civil rights movement. In an immediate sense, it triggered an explosion of pain, frustration, and violence. Angry and retaliatory, black mobs in many American cities burned and ransacked homes and businesses. More significantly, however, the assassination of Martin Luther King Jr., coupled with the rise of more militant groups and their opposing agendas, led to the dissolution of what had been a unified quest for civil rights.

As the civil rights movement lost momentum during the late 1960s, even the more radical organizations began to wane. Although many groups and organizations that had peaked during the civil rights era continued to operate, the moral outrage and sense of a common cause that had fueled the movement dissipated.

The civil rights movement resulted in many positive gains for blacks, most notably the abolishment of Jim Crow barriers. Due to expanded voting rights, for example, many blacks have been elected to local, state, and national offices. Much progress, too, has been made in the economic sector, largely as a result of increased access to education and economic opportunity. At the same time, however, a disproportionately high number of black Americans remained trapped in urban poverty and a cycle of economic woes. Police brutality against African Americans is another issue that commands frequent attention.

As the twenty-first century unfolds, the struggle to address these and other racial problems will continue to define America. Although Martin Luther King Jr. did not live to see all of his goals met, his prophetic statement that "injustice anywhere is a threat to justice everywhere" reverberates today as minority groups continue to strive for full equality.

CHAPTER ONE

GREAT
SPEECHES
IN
HISTORY

Civil Rights Pioneers

What to the Slave Is the Fourth of July?

Frederick Douglass

Frederick Douglass was America's foremost black leader of the 1800s. Born into slavery on a Maryland farm in 1818, Douglass managed to escape to the North when he was twenty years old. In New England Douglass became the leading spokesman of the Anti-Slavery Society and later founded the *North Star*, a newspaper that promoted black rights—and democratic ideals in general. His skills as an orator and his unflagging devotion to abolitionist causes attracted enthusiastic supporters wherever he went.

In 1852 the Rochester Ladies' Anti-Slavery Society asked Douglass to speak during the city's Fourth of July celebrations. Douglass obliged, but used the occasion to denounce the hypocrisy of a nation trumpeting the principles of freedom and liberty while at the same time enslaving millions of African Americans. As Douglass pointedly reminds his audience, "The rich inheritance of justice, liberty, prosperity and independence, bequeathed by your fathers, is shared by you, not by me."

Fellow citizens, pardon me, allow me to ask, why am I called upon to speak here today? What have I, or those I represent, to do with your national independence? Are the great principles of political freedom and of natural justice, embodied in that Declaration of Independence, extended to us? and am I, therefore, called upon to bring our humble offering to the national altar, and to confess the ben-

Excerpted from Frederick Douglass's speech in Rochester, New York, July 5, 1852.

efits and express devout gratitude for the blessings resulting from your independence to us?

Would to God, both for your sakes and ours, that an affirmative answer could be truthfully returned to these questions! Then would my task be light, and my burden easy and delightful. For who is there so cold, that a nation's sympathy could not warm him? Who so obdurate and dead to the claims of gratitude, that would not thankfully acknowledge such priceless benefits? Who so stolid and selfish, that would not give his voice to swell the hallelujahs of a nation's jubilee, when the chains of servitude had been torn from his limbs? I am not that man. In a case like that, the dumb might eloquently speak, and the "lame man leap as an hart."

But, such is not the state of the case. I say it with a sad sense of the disparity between us. I am not included within the pale of this glorious anniversary! Your high independence only reveals the immeasurable distance between us. The blessings in which you, this day, rejoice, are not enjoyed in common. The rich inheritance of justice, liberty, prosperity and independence, bequeathed by your fathers, is shared by you, not by me. The sunlight that brought life and healing to you, has brought stripes and death to me. This Fourth [of] July is yours, not mine. You may rejoice, I must mourn. To drag a man in fetters into the grand illuminated temple of liberty, and call upon him to join you in joyous anthems, were inhuman mockery and sacrilegious irony. Do you mean, citizens, to mock me, by asking me to speak today? If so, there is a parallel to your conduct. And let me warn you that it is dangerous to copy the example of a nation whose crimes, lowering up to heaven, were thrown down by the breath of the Almighty, burying that nation in irrecoverable ruin! I can today take up the plaintive lament of a peeled and woe-smitten people!

"By the rivers of Babylon, there we sat down. Yea! we wept when we remembered Zion. We hanged our harps upon the willows in the midst thereof. For there, they that carried us away captive, required of us a song; and they who wasted us required of us mirth, saying, Sing us one of the songs of Zion. How can we sing the Lord's song in a strange land? If I forget thee, O Jerusalem, let my right hand forget her cunning. If I do not remember thee, let my tongue cleave to the roof of my mouth."

A Slave's Point of View

Fellow citizens; above your national, tumultous joy, I hear the mournful wail of millions, whose chains, heavy and grievous yesterday, are, today, rendered more intolerable by the jubilant shouts that reach them. If I do forget, if I do not faithfully remember those bleeding children of sorrow this day, "may my right hand forget her cunning, and may my tongue cleave to the roof of my mouth!" To forget them, to pass lightly over their wrongs, and to chime in with the popular theme, would be treason most scandalous and shocking, and would make me a reproach before God and the world. My subject, then, fellow citizens, is AMERICAN SLAVERY. I shall see, this day, and its popular characteristics, from the slave's point of view. Standing here, identified with the American bondman, making his wrongs mine, I do not hesitate to declare, with all my soul, that the character and conduct of this nation never looked blacker to me than on this Fourth of July! Whether we turn to the declarations of the past, or to the professions of the present, the conduct of the nation seems equally hideous and revolting. America is false to the past, false to the present, and solemnly binds herself to be false to the future. Standing with God and the crushed and bleeding slave on this occasion, I will, in the name of humanity which is outraged, in the name of liberty which is fettered, in the name of the constitution and the Bible, which are disregarded and trampled upon, dare to call in question and to denounce, with all the emphasis I can command, everything that serves to perpetuate slavery—the great sin and shame of America! "I will not equivocate; I will not excuse;" I will use the severest language I can command; and yet not one word shall escape me that any man, whose judgement is not blinded by prejudice, or who is not at heart a slaveholder, shall not confess to be right and just.

But I fancy I hear some one of my audience say, it is just in this circumstance that you and your brother abolitionists fail to make a favorable impression on the public mind.

Would you argue more, and denounce less, would you persuade more, and rebuke less, your cause would be much more likely to succeed. But, I submit, where all is plain there is nothing to be argued. What point in the anti-slavery creed would you have me argue? On what branch of the subject do the people of this country need light? Must I undertake to prove that the slave is a man? That point is conceded already. Nobody doubts it. The slaveholders themselves acknowledge it in the enactment of laws for their government. They acknowledge it when they punish disobedience on the part of the slave. There are seventy-two crimes in the State of Virginia, which, if committed by a black man (no matter how ignorant he be), subject him to the punishment of death; while only two of the same crimes will subject a white man to the like punishment. What is this but the acknowledgment that the slave is a

Frederick Douglass

moral, intellectual and responsible being? The manhood of the slave is conceded. It is admitted in the fact that Southern statute books are covered with enactments forbidding, under severe fines and penalties, the teaching of the slave to read or to write. When you can point to any such laws, in reference to the beasts of the field, then I may consent to argue the manhood of the slave. When the dogs in your streets, when the fowls of the air, when the cattle on your hills, when the fish of the sea, and the reptiles that crawl, shall be unable to distinguish the slave from a brute, then will I argue with you that the slave is a man!

For the present, it is enough to affirm the equal manhood of the negro race. Is it not astonishing that, while we are ploughing, planting and reaping, using all kinds of mechanical tools, erecting houses, constructing bridges, building ships, working in metals of brass, iron, copper, silver and gold; that, while we are reading, writing and cyphering, acting as clerks, merchants and secretaries, having among us lawyers, doctors, ministers, poets, authors, editors, orators and teachers; that, while we are engaged in all manner of enterprises common to other men, digging gold in California, capturing the whale in the Pacific, feeding sheep and cattle on the hillside, living, moving, acting, thinking, planning, living in families as husbands, wives and children, and, above all, confessing and worshipping the Christian's God, and looking hopefully for life and immortality beyond the grave, we are called upon to prove that we are men!

Would you have me argue that man is entitled to liberty? That he is the rightful owner of his own body? You have already declared it. Must I argue the wrongfulness of slavery? Is that a question for Republicans? Is it to be settled by the rules of logic and argumentation, as a matter beset with great difficulty, involving a doubtful application of the principle of justice, hard to be understood? How should I look today, in the presence of Americans, dividing, and subdividing a discourse, to show that men have a natural right to freedom, speaking of it relatively, and positively, negatively, and affirmatively? To do so, would be to make myself ridiculous, and to offer an insult to your understanding. There is not a man beneath the canopy of heaven, that does not know that slavery is wrong for him.

What, am I to argue that it is wrong to make men brutes, to rob them of their liberty, to work them without wages, to keep them ignorant of their relations to their fellow men, to beat them with sticks, to flay their flesh with the lash, to load their limbs with irons, to hunt them with dogs, to sell them at auction, to sunder their families, to knock out their teeth, to burn their flesh, to starve them into obedience and submission to their masters? Must I argue that a system thus marked with blood and stained with pollution, is wrong? No! I will not. I have better employments for my time and strength, than such arguments would imply.

What, then, remains to be argued? Is it that slavery is not divine; that God did not establish it; that our doctors of divinity are mistaken? There is blasphemy in the thought. That which is inhuman cannot be divine! Who can reason on such a proposition? They that can, may; I cannot. The time for such argument is past.

At a time like this, scorching irony, not convincing argument, is needed. O! had I the ability, and could I reach the nation's ear, I would, today, pour out a fiery stream of biting ridicule, blasting reproach, withering sarcasm, and stern rebuke. For it is not light that is needed, but fire; it is not the gentle shower, but thunder. We need the storm, the whirlwind, and the earthquake. The feeling of the nation must be quickened; the conscience of the nation must be roused; the propriety of the nation must be startled; the hypocrisy of the nation must be exposed; and its crimes against God and man must be proclaimed and denounced.

The Shame of Slavery

What, to the American slave, is your Fourth of July? I answer: a day that reveals to him, more than all other days in the year, the gross injustice and cruelty to which he is the constant victim. To him, your celebration is a sham; your boasted liberty, an unholy license; your national greatness, swelling vanity; your sounds of rejoicing are empty and heartless; your denunciations of tyrants, brass fronted impudence; your shouts of liberty and equality, hollow mockery; your prayers and hymns, your sermons and thanksgivings, with all your religious parade and solemnity, are, to him, mere bombast, fraud, deception, impiety, and hypocrisy—a thin veil to cover up crimes which would disgrace a nation of savages. There is not a nation on the earth guilty of practices, more shocking and bloody, than are the people of these United States, at this very hour.

Go where you may, search where you will, roam through all the monarchies and despotisms of the old world, travel through South America, search out every abuse, and when you have found the last, lay your facts by the side of the everyday practices of this nation, and you will say with me, that, for revolting barbarity and shameless hypocrisy, America reigns without a rival.

Equality Through Education and Self-Improvement

Booker T. Washington

Booker T. Washington was the most influential leader of black America at the turn of the nineteenth century. Born into slavery on a Virginia farm in 1856, Washington had just turned nine years old when the Civil War ended and he attained his freedom. In 1881 he founded the Tuskegee Institute, a vocational school that advocated industrial and agricultural training for blacks. His success as an educator and his highly regarded work ethic brought Washington wide recognition.

In 1895 Washington was invited to address an audience of several thousand at the Cotton States and International Exposition in Atlanta, Georgia. In his speech, reprinted here, Washington calls for blacks to postpone forceful attempts to secure civil rights. Rather, Washington exhorts blacks to uplift themselves through education, self-improvement, and economic self-reliance. Although Washington's policy of accommodation on racial issues was accepted enthusiastically by white society, it divided many in the black community who advocated more aggressive legal and political action as a means to secure civil rights. Its checkered reception notwithstanding, this speech not only set the tone for race policy as the twentieth century unfolded, it also marked Washington as America's leading black spokesman.

From Booker T. Washington's speech at the Atlanta Cotton States and International Exposition, Atlanta, Georgia, September 18, 1895.

Mr. President and Gentlemen of the Board of Directors and Citizens:
One-third of the population of the South is of the Negro race. No enterprise seeking the material, civil, or moral welfare of this section can disregard this element of our population and reach the highest success. I but convey to you, Mr. President and Directors, the sentiment of the masses of my race when I say that in no way have the value and manhood of the American Negro been more fittingly and generously recognized than by the managers of this magnificent Exposition at every stage of its progress. It is a recognition that will do more to cement the friendship of the two races than any occurrence since the dawn of our freedom.

Not only this, but the opportunity here afforded will awaken among us a new era of industrial progress. Ignorant and inexperienced, it is not strange that in the first years of our new life we began at the top instead of at the bottom; that a seat in Congress or the state legislature was more sought than real estate or industrial skill; that the political convention or stump speaking had more attractions than starting a dairy farm or truck garden.

A ship lost at sea for many days suddenly sighted a friendly vessel. From the mast of the unfortunate vessel was seen a signal, "Water, water; we die of thirst!" The answer from the friendly vessel at once came back, "Cast down your bucket where you are." A second time the signal, "Water, water; send us water!" ran up from the distressed vessel, and was answered, "Cast down your bucket where you are." And a third and fourth signal for water was answered, "Cast down your bucket where you are." The captain of the distressed vessel, at last heeding the injunction, cast down his bucket, and it came up full of fresh, sparkling water from the mouth of the Amazon River.

Cultivating Friendly Relations

To those of my race who depend on bettering their condition in a foreign land or who underestimate the importance of cultivating friendly relations with the Southern white man, who is their next-door neighbor, I would say: "Cast down your bucket where you are"—cast it down in making friends in every manly way of the people of all races by whom we are surrounded.

Cast it down in agriculture, mechanics, in commerce, in domestic service, and in the professions. And in this connection it is well to bear in mind that whatever other sins the South may be called to bear, when it comes to business, pure and simple, it is in the South that the Negro is given a man's chance in the commercial world, and in nothing is this Exposition more eloquent than in emphasizing this chance. Our greatest danger is that in the great leap from slavery to freedom we may overlook the fact that the masses of us are to live by the productions of our hands, and fail to keep in mind that we shall prosper in proportion as we learn to dignify and glorify common labor, and put brains and skill into the common occupations of life; shall prosper in proportion as we learn to draw the line between the superficial and the substantial, the ornamental gewgaws of life and the useful. No race can prosper till it learns that there is as much dignity in tilling a field as in writing a poem. It is at the bottom of life we must begin, and not at the top. Nor should we permit our grievances to overshadow our opportunities.

"Cast Down Your Bucket Where You Are!"

To those of the white race who look to the incoming of those of foreign birth and strange tongue and habits for the prosperity of the South, were I permitted I would repeat what I say to my own race, "Cast down your bucket where you are." Cast it down among the eight millions of Negroes whose habits you know, whose fidelity and love you have tested in days when to have proved treacherous meant the ruin of your firesides. Cast down your bucket among these people who have, without strikes and labor wars, tilled your fields, cleared your forests, builded your railroads and cities, and brought forth treasures from the bowels of the earth, and helped make possible this magnificent representation of the progress of the South. Casting down your bucket among my people, helping and encouraging them as you are doing

on these grounds, and to education of head, hand, and heart, you will find that they will buy your surplus land, make blossom the waste places in your fields, and run your factories. While doing this, you can be sure in the future, as in the past, that you and your families will be surrounded by the most patient, faithful, law-abiding, and unresentful people that the world has seen. As we have proved our loyalty to you in the past, in nursing your children, watching by the sick-bed of your mothers and fathers, and often following them with tear-dimmed eyes to their graves, so in the future, in our humble way, we shall stand by you with a devotion that no foreigner can approach, ready to lay down our lives, if need be, in defense of yours, interlacing our industrial, commercial, civil, and religious life with yours in a way that shall make the interests of both races one. In all things that are purely social, we can be as separate as the fingers, yet one as the hand in all things essential to mutual progress.

There is no defense or security for any of us except in the highest intelligence and development of all. If anywhere there are efforts tending to curtail the fullest growth of the Negro, let these efforts be turned into stimulating, encouraging, and making him the most useful and intelligent citizen. Effort or

Influential civil rights leader Booker T. Washington addresses a large crowd.

means so invested will pay a thousand percent interest. These efforts will be twice blessed—blessing him that gives and him that takes.

There is no escape through law of man or God from the inevitable:

> The laws of changeless justice bind
> Oppressor with oppressed;
> And close as sin and suffering joined
> We march to fate abreast.

Nearly sixteen millions of hands will aid you in pulling the load upward, or they will pull against you the load downward. We shall constitute one-third and more of the ignorance and crime of the South, or one-third its intelligence and progress; we shall contribute one-third to the business and industrial prosperity of the South, or we shall prove a veritable body of death, stagnating, depressing, retarding every effort to advance the body politic.

Gentlemen of the Exposition, as we present to you our humble effort at an exhibition of our progress, you must not expect overmuch. Starting thirty years ago with ownership here and there in a few quilts and pumpkins and chickens (gathered from miscellaneous sources), remember the path that has led from these to the inventions and production of agricultural implements, buggies, steam-engines, newspapers, books, statuary, carving, paintings, the management of drug stores and banks, has not been trodden without contact with thorns and thistles.

Hope and Encouragement

While we take pride in what we exhibit as a result of our independent efforts, we do not for a moment forget that our part in this exhibition would fall far short of your expectations but for the constant help that has come to our educational life, not only from the Southern states, but especially from northern philanthropists, who have made their gifts a constant stream of blessing and encouragement.

The wisest among my race understand that the agitation of questions of social equality is the extremist folly, and that progress in the enjoyment of all the privileges that will come to us must be the result of severe and constant struggle rather than of artificial forcing. No race that has anything to contribute to the markets of the world is long in any degree ostracized. It is important and right that all privileges of the law be ours, but it is vastly more important that we be prepared for the exercise of these privileges. The opportunity to earn a dollar in a factory just now is worth infinitely more than the opportunity to spend a dollar in an opera-house.

In conclusion, may I repeat that nothing in thirty years has given us more hope and encouragement, and drawn us so near to you of the white race, as this opportunity offered by the Exposition; and here bending, as it were, over the altar that represents the results of the struggles of your race and mine, both starting practically empty-handed three decades ago, I pledge that in your effort to work out the great and intricate problem which God has laid at the doors of the South, you shall have at all times the patient, sympathetic help of my race; only let this be constantly in mind, that, while from representations in these buildings of the product of field, of forest, of mine, of factory, letters, and art, much good will come, yet far above and beyond material benefits will be that higher good, that, let us pray God, will come, in a blotting out of sectional differences and racial animosities and suspicions, in a determination to administer absolute justice, in a willing obedience among all classes to the mandates of law.

This, coupled with our material prosperity, will bring into our beloved South a new heaven and a new earth.

A Demand for Equal Rights

W.E.B. Du Bois

Civil rights activist and one of America's most distinguished scholars, W.E.B. Du Bois began his long career in the public spotlight when in 1895 he became the first African American to receive a Ph.D. degree from Harvard University. In the struggle for black rights, Du Bois rallied Americans to attack, through legal and political action, a cadre of injustices that affected the black community—inequalities in education and law enforcement, for example. At the same time, he remained a vocal opponent of Booker T. Washington and others who preached less strident and more tolerant means of promoting black rights.

In 1905 Du Bois and several other black leaders met at Niagara Falls to organize and publicize their demands for basic civil rights. This conference became known as the Niagara Movement, and although it would disband within five years, it sowed the seeds for what would become the nucleus of the National Association for the Advancement of Colored People. In his address at the second Niagara Conference, reprinted here, Du Bois enumerates specific goals of the movement—most compellingly complete and equal rights for all Americans. To this end, Du Bois pointedly urges every American to take an active role in securing basic constitutional rights and privileges—and to protest loudly when these rights are denied.

From W.E.B. Du Bois's speech at the Second Annual Meeting of the Niagara Conference, Harpers Ferry, West Virginia, August 16, 1906.

The men of the Niagara Movement coming from the toil of the year's hard work and pausing a moment from the earning of their daily bread turn toward the nation and again ask, in the name of ten million, the privilege of a hearing.

In the past year the work of the Negro-hater has flourished in the land. Step by step the defenders of the rights of American citizens have retreated. The work of stealing the black man's ballot has progressed and the fifty and more representatives of stolen votes still sit in the nation's capital. Discrimination in travel and public accommodation has so spread that some of our weaker brethren are actually afraid to thunder against color discrimination as such and are simply whispering for ordinary decencies. Against this the Niagara Movement eternally protests. We will not be satisfied to take one jot or tittle less than our full manhood rights!

A Fight for Ideals

We claim for ourselves every single right that belongs to a freeborn American, political, civil and social; and until we get these rights we will never cease to protest and assail the ears of America! The battle we wage is not for ourselves alone but for all true Americans. It is a fight for ideals, lest this, our common fatherland, false to its founding, become in truth, the land of the thief and the home of the slave, a byword and a hissing among the nations for its sounding pretensions and pitiful accomplishments.

Never before in the modern age has a great and civilized folk threatened to adopt so cowardly a creed in the treatment of its fellow citizens born and bred on its soil. Stripped of verbiage and subterfuge and in its naked nastiness, the new American creed says: "Fear to let black men even try to rise lest they become the equals of the white." And this is the land that professes to follow Jesus Christ! The blasphemy of such a course is only matched by its cowardice.

Unequivocal Demands

In detail, our demands are clear and unequivocal. First, we would vote; with the right to vote goes everything: freedom, manhood, the honor of your wives, the chastity of your daughters, the right to work, and the chance to rise, and let no man listen to those who deny this.

We want full manhood suffrage, and we want it now, henceforth and forever!

Second. We want discrimination in public accommodation to cease. Separation in railway and street cars, based simply on race and color, is un-American, undemocratic, and silly.

Third. We claim the right of freemen to walk, talk, and be with them that wish to be with us. No man has a right to choose another man's friends, and to attempt to do so is an impudent interference with the most fundamental human privilege.

Fourth. We want the laws enforced against rich as well as poor; against capitalist as well as laborer; against white as well as black. We are not more lawless than the white race: We are more

W.E.B. Du Bois

often arrested, convicted and mobbed. We want Congress to take charge of Congressional elections. We want the Fourteenth Amendment carried out to the letter and every state disfranchised in Congress which attempts to disfranchise its rightful voters. We want the Fifteenth Amendment enforced and no state allowed to base its franchise simply on color.

The failure of the Republican Party in Congress at the session just closed to redeem its pledge . . . to suffrage conditions in the South seems a plain, deliberate, and premeditated breach of promise, and stamps that Party as guilty of obtaining votes under false pretense.

Fifth. We want our children educated. The school system in the country districts of the South is a disgrace, and in few towns and cities are the Negro schools what they ought to be. We want the national government to step in and wipe out illiteracy in the South. Either the United States will destroy ignorance, or ignorance will destroy the United States.

And when we call for education we mean real education. We believe in work. We ourselves are workers, but work is not necessarily education. Education is the development of power and ideal. We want our children trained as intelligent human beings should be, and we will fight for all time against any proposal to educate black boys and girls simply as servants and underlings, or simply for the use of other people. They have a right to know, to think, to aspire.

These are some of the chief things which we want. How shall we get them? By voting where we may vote, by persistent, unceasing agitation, by hammering at the truth, by sacrifice and work.

The Spirit of John Brown

We do not believe in violence, neither in the despised violence of the raid nor the lauded violence of the soldier, nor the barbarous violence of the mob, but we do believe in John Brown, in that incarnate spirit of justice, that hatred of a lie, that willingness to sacrifice money, reputation, and life itself on the altar of right. And here on the scene of John Brown's martyrdom, we reconsecrate ourselves, our honor, our property to the final emancipation of the race which John Brown died to make free.

Our enemies, triumphant for the present, are fighting the stars in their courses. Justice and humanity must prevail. We live to tell these dark brothers of ours—scattered in counsel, wavering, and weak—that no bribe of money or notoriety, no promise of wealth or fame, is worth the surrender of a people's manhood or the loss of a man's self-respect. We refuse to surrender the leadership of this race to cowards and trucklers. We are men; we will be treated as men. On this rock we have planted our banners. We will never give up, though the trump of doom finds us still fighting.

And we shall win! The past promised it. The present foretells it. Thank God for John Brown. Thank God for Garrison and Douglass, Sumner and Phillips, Nat Turner and Robert Gould Shaw, and all the hallowed dead who died for freedom. Thank God for all those today, few though their voices be, who have not forgotten the divine brotherhood of all men, white and black, rich and poor, fortunate and unfortunate.

We appeal to the young men and women of this nation, to those whose nostrils are not yet befouled by greed and snobbery and racial narrowness: Stand up for the right, prove yourselves worthy of your heritage and, whether born North or South, dare to treat men as men. Cannot the nation that has absorbed ten-million foreigners into its political life without catastrophe absorb ten-million Negro Americans into that same political life at less cost than their unjust and illegal exclusion will involve?

Signs of Promise

Courage, brothers! The battle for humanity is not lost or losing. All across the skies sit signs of promise! [DuBois points skyward.] The Slav is rising in his might, the yellow millions are tasting liberty, the black Africans are writhing toward the light, and everywhere the laborer, with ballot in his hand, is voting open the gates of opportunity and peace.

The morning breaks over blood-stained hills. We must not falter, we may not shrink.

Above are the everlasting stars.

On Being a Black Woman

Mary Church Terrell

Mary Church Terrell was a popular speaker and writer. She is remembered not only for her efforts to further feminist causes, but also for her many speeches and articles that denounced segregation. Terrell was born in 1863, a time when most blacks lived in abject poverty in the rural South. In contrast, Terrell was raised in a wealthy family that afforded her many educational opportunities. Despite her affluence, Terrell was not immune to the sting of discrimination, and, after a distinguished teaching career, Terrell joined the fight for equal rights.

As the first president of the National Association of Colored Women and a founding member of the National Association for the Advancement of Colored People, Terrell toured lecture circuits across the nation, voicing her opposition to racial segregation. In this 1906 speech to the United Women's Club in Washington, D.C., Terrell presents a litany of anecdotes that illustrate the hardships that black Americans were forced to endure. In her moving testimony, Terrell concludes that "nowhere in the world do oppression and persecution based solely on the color of the skin appear more hateful and hideous than in the capital of the United States."

Washington, D.C., has been called "The Colored Man's Paradise." Whether this sobriquet was given to the national capital in bitter irony by a member of the handicapped race, as he reviewed some of his own per-

Excerpted from Mary Church Terrell's speech to the United Women's Club, Washington, DC, October 10, 1906.

secutions and rebuffs, or whether it was given immediately after the war by an ex-slaveholder who for the first time in his life saw colored people walking about like free men, minus the overseer and his whip, history saith not. It is certain that it would be difficult to find a worse misnomer for Washington than "The Colored Man's Paradise" if so prosaic a consideration as veracity is to determine the appropriateness of a name.

Intolerable Conditions

For fifteen years I have resided in Washington, and while it was far from being a paradise for colored people when I first touched these shores, it has been doing its level best ever since to make conditions for us intolerable. As a colored woman I might enter Washington any night, a stranger in a strange land, and walk miles without finding a place to lay my head. Unless I happened to know colored people who live here or ran across a chance acquaintance who could recommend a colored boarding-house to me, I should be obliged to spend the entire night wandering about. Indians, Chinamen, Filipinos, Japanese and representatives of any other dark race can find hotel accommodations, if they can pay for them. The colored man alone is thrust out of the hotels of the national capital like a leper . . .

As a colored woman I cannot visit the tomb of the Father of this Country, which owes its very existence to the love of freedom in the human heart and which stands for equal opportunity to all, without being forced to sit in the Jim Crow section of an electric car which starts from the very heart of the city—midway between the Capitol and the White House. If I refuse thus to be humiliated, I am cast into jail and forced to pay a fine for violating the Virginia laws . . .

As a colored woman I may enter more than one white church in Washington without receiving that welcome which as a human being I have a right to expect in the sanctuary of God. Sometimes the color blindness of the usher takes on that peculiar form which prevents a dark face from making any impression whatsoever upon his retina, so that it is impossible for him to see colored people at all. If he is not so afflicted, after keeping a colored man or woman waiting a long time, he will ungraciously show these dusky Christians who have had the temerity to thrust themselves into a temple where only the fair of face are expected to worship God to a seat in the rear, which is named in honor of a certain personage, well known in this country, and commonly called Jim Crow.

Employment Discrimination

Unless I am willing to engage in a few menial occupations, in which the pay for my services would be very poor, there is no way for me to earn an honest living, if I am not a trained nurse or a dressmaker or can secure a position as a teacher in the public schools, which is exceedingly difficult to do. It matters not what my intellectual attainments may be or how great is the need of the services of a competent person, if I try to enter many of the numerous vocations in which my white sisters are allowed to engage, the door is shut in my face.

From one Washington theater I am excluded altogether . . . [After explaining that] in some of the theaters colored nurses were allowed to sit with the white children for whom they cared, the ticket seller told me that in Washington it was very poor policy to employ colored nurses, for they were excluded from many places where white girls would be allowed to take children for pleasure.

If I possess artistic talent, there is not a single art school of repute which will admit me. A few years ago a colored woman who possessed great talent submitted some drawings to the Corcoran Art School, of Washington, which were accepted by the committee of awards, who sent her a ticket entitling her to a course in this school. But when the committee discovered that the young woman was colored, they declined to admit her, and told her that if they had suspected that her drawings had been made by a colored woman, they would not have examined them at all . . .

With the exception of the Catholic University, there is not a single white college in the national capital to which colored people are admitted, no matter how great their ability, how lofty their ambition, how unexceptionable their character or how great their thirst for knowledge may be. A few years ago the Columbian Law School [in Washington] admitted colored students, but in deference to the Southern white students the authorities have decided to exclude them altogether . . .

Discrimination Based on Skin Color

Another young friend, in order to secure lucrative employment, left Washington and went to New York. There she worked her way up in one of the largest dry goods stores till she was placed as saleswoman in the cloak department. Tired of being separated from her family, she decided to return to Washington, feeling sure that, with her experience and her fine recommendation from the New York firm, she could easily secure employment. Nor was she overconfident, for the proprietor of one of the largest dry goods stores in her native city was glad to secure the services of a young woman who brought such hearty credentials from New York. She had not been in this store very long, however, before she called upon me one day and asked me to intercede with the proprietor in her behalf, saying that she had been discharged that afternoon because it had been discovered that she was colored.

When I called upon my young friend's employer, he made no effort to avoid the issue, as I feared he would. He did not say he had discharged the young saleswoman because she had not given satisfaction, as he might easily have done. On the contrary, he admitted without the slightest hesitation that the young woman he had just discharged was one of the best clerks he had ever had. In the cloak department, where she had been assigned, she had been a brilliant success, he said. "But I cannot keep Miss Smith in my employ," he concluded. "Are you not master of your own store?" I ventured to inquire. The proprietor of this store was a Jew, and I felt that it was particularly cruel, unnatural and cold blooded for the representative of one oppressed and persecuted race to deal so harshly and unjustly with a member of another. I had intended to make this point when I decided to intercede for my young friend, but when I thought how a reference to the persecution of his own race would wound his feelings, the words froze on my lips. "When I first heard your friend was colored," he explained, "I did not believe it and said so to the clerks who made the statement. Finally, the girls who had been most pronounced in their opposition to working in a store with a colored girl came to me in a body and threatened to strike. 'Strike away,' said I, 'your places will be easily filled.' Then they started on another tack. Delegation after delegation began to file down to my office, some of the women my very best customers, to protest against my employing a colored girl. Moreover, they threatened to boycott my store if I did not discharge her at once. Then it became a question of bread and butter, and I yielded to the inevitable— that's all. Now," said he, concluding, "if I lived in a great, cosmopolitan city like New York, I should do as I pleased, and refuse to discharge a girl simply because she was colored."

But I thought of a similar incident that happened in New York. I remembered that a colored woman, as fair as a lily and as beautiful as a Madonna, who was the head saleswoman in a large department store in New York, had been discharged, after she had held this position for years, when the proprietor accidentally discovered that a fatal drop of African blood was percolating somewhere through her veins . . .

A Young Victim of Oppression

Not long ago one of my little daughter's bosom friends figured in one of the most pathetic instances of which I have ever heard. A gentleman who is very fond of children promised to take six little girls in his neighborhood to a matinee. It happened that he himself and five of his little friends were so fair that they easily passed muster, as they stood in judgment before the ticket seller and the ticket taker. Three of the little girls were sisters, two of whom were very fair and the other a bit brown. Just as this little girl, who happened to be last in the procession, went by the ticket taker, that Argus-eyed, sophisticated gentleman detected something which caused a deep, dark frown to mantle his brow and he did not allow her to pass. "I guess you have made a mistake," he called to the host of this theater party. "Those little girls," pointing to the fair ones, "may be admitted, but this one," designating the brown one, "can't." But the colored man was quite equal to the emergency. Fairly frothing at the mouth with anger, he asked the ticket taker what he meant, what he was trying to insinuate about that particular little girl. "Do you mean to tell me," he shouted in rage, "that I must go clear to the Philippine Islands to bring this child to the United States, and then I can't take her to the theater in the national capital?" The little ruse succeeded brilliantly, as he knew it would. "Beg your pardon," said the ticket taker, "don't know what I was thinking about. Of course she can go in."

"What was the matter with me this afternoon, mother?" asked the little brown girl innocently, when she mentioned the affair at home. "Why did the man at the theater let my two sisters and the other girls in and try to keep me out?" In relating this incident, the child's mother told me her little girl's question, which showed such blissful ignorance of the depressing, cruel conditions which confronted her, completely unnerved her for a time.

Prejudice Against Teachers

Although white and colored teachers are under the same Board of Education, and the system for the children of both races is said to be uniform, prejudice against the colored teachers in the public schools is manifested in a variety of ways. From 1870 to 1900 there was a colored superintendent at the head of the colored schools. During all that time the directors of the cooking, sewing, physical culture, manual training, music and art departments were colored people. Six years ago a change was inaugurated. The colored superintendent was legislated out of office, and the directorships, without a single exception, were taken from colored teachers and given to the whites. There was no complaint about the work done by the colored directors, no more than is heard about every officer in every school. The directors of the art and physical culture departments were particularly fine. Now, no matter how competent or superior the colored teachers in our public schools may be, they know that they can never rise to the height of a directorship, can never hope to be more than an assistant and receive the meager salary therefore, unless the present regime is radically changed.

Not long ago one of the most distinguished [kindergarten directors] in the country came to deliver a course of lectures in Washington. The colored teachers were eager to attend, but they could not buy the coveted privilege for love or money. When they appealed to [their supervisor], they were told that the expert kindergartner had come to Washington under the auspices of private individuals, so that she could not possibly have them admitted. Realizing what a loss colored teachers had sustained in being deprived of the information and inspiration which these lectures afforded, one of the white teachers volunteered to repeat them as best she could for the benefit of her colored co-laborers for half the price she herself had paid, and the proposition was eagerly accepted by some. . . .

I might go on citing instance after instance to show the variety of ways in which our people are sacrificed on the altar of prejudice in the capital of the United States and how almost insurmountable are the obstacles which block our paths to success. Early in life many a colored youth is so appalled by the helplessness and the hopelessness of his situation in this country that, in a sort of stoical despair he resigns himself to his fate. "What is the good of our trying to acquire an education? We can't all be preachers, teachers, doctors and lawyers. Besides those professions, there is almost nothing for colored people to do but engage in the most menial occupations, and we do not need an education for that." More than once such remarks, uttered by young men and women in our public schools who possess brilliant intellects, have wrung my heart.

It is impossible for any white person in the United States, no matter how sympathetic and broadminded, to realize what life would mean to him if his incentive to effort were suddenly snatched away. To the lack of incentive to effort, which is the awful shadow under which we live, may be traced the wreck and ruin of scores of colored youth. And surely nowhere in the world do oppression and persecution based solely on the color of the skin appear more hateful and hideous than in the capital of the United States, because the chasm between the principles upon which this Government was founded, in which it still professes to believe, and those which are daily practiced under the protection of the flag, yawns so wide and deep.

Goals of the Civil Rights Movement

Racial Separation

Malcolm X

The terms *black power* and *black nationalism* came into popularity during the sixties as many frustrated blacks grew disillusioned with the gains made by the civil rights movement. Black power, which stood for black pride and self-determination, reflected a rift in the black community between those who sought peaceful integration and those who advocated not only more militant methods of securing their freedom, but also complete separation from white society. While several well-known civil rights activists espoused this latter view, the Muslim leader Malcolm X is remembered as one of the most compelling voices calling for the establishment of a black nation.

Born Malcolm Little, Malcolm changed his name when, while serving a prison sentence, he became a follower of Elijah Muhammad, the leader of the Nation of Islam. Upon his parole in 1952, Malcolm X himself became a leader of the Black Muslim movement. His fiery oratory and plea for black pride attracted many followers, although his forceful personality and militant views led ultimately to his expulsion from the Black Muslim movement in 1963. In his speeches and writings, Malcolm X urged blacks to band together, celebrate their heritage, and reject white America—contending that blacks should use any means necessary to achieve these goals. Because his approach to race relations did not rule out violence, many condemned his views as too extreme and ultimately dangerous. In October 1963, Malcolm X spoke at the University of California at Berkeley. In his speech, reprinted here, Malcolm X explains why blacks should reject the goal of integration and instead push to establish a black homeland.

Excerpted from Malcolm X's speech at the University of California at Berkeley, October 11, 1963.

Our people in the Negro community are trapped in a vicious cycle of ignorance, poverty, disease, sickness, and death. There seems to be no way out. No way of escape. The wealthy, educated Black bourgeoisie, those up-pity Negroes who do escape, never reach back and pull the rest of our people out with them. The Black masses remain trapped in the slums.

And because there seems to be no hope or no other escape, we turn to wine, we turn to whiskey, and we turn to reefers, marijuana, and even to the dreadful needle—heroin, morphine, cocaine, opium—seeking an escape.

Many of us turn to crime, stealing, gambling, prostitution. And some of us are used by the white overlords downtown to push dope in the Negro community among our own people. Unemployment and poverty have forced many of our people into a life of crime. But the real criminal is in the City Hall downtown, in the State House, and in the White House in Washington, D.C. The real criminal is the white liberal, the political hypocrite. And it is these legal crooks who pose as our friends, force us into a life of crime, and then use us to spread the white man's evil vices in our community among our own people.

The Honorable Elijah Muhammad teaches us that our people are scientifically maneuvered by the white man into a life of poverty. Because we are forced to live in the poorest sections of the city, we attend inferior schools. We have inferior teachers and we get an inferior education. The white power structure downtown makes certain that by the time our people do graduate, we won't be equipped or qualified for anything but the dirtiest, heaviest, poorest-paying jobs. Jobs that no one else wants.

We are trapped in a vicious cycle of economic, intellectual, social, and political death. Inferior jobs, inferior housing, inferior education which in turn again leads to inferior jobs. We spend a lifetime in this vicious circle. Or in this vicious cycle going in circles. Giving birth to children who see no hope or future but to follow in our miserable footsteps.

So we thank God for the Honorable Elijah Muhammad. We who are Muslims saw no way out until we accepted the religion of Islam and the spiritual guidance of the Honorable

Elijah Muhammad. We saw no solution to our problems. We saw no real leader among our people.

But today the whole world is talking about the Honorable Elijah Muhammad and the divine solution he received from the God of our forefathers. Not your God but from the God of our forefathers. Not a temporary solution which will benefit only the handpicked upper-class Negroes, but a solution divinely designed to solve the plight of the Black masses in this country permanently and forever.

Token Integration

The government does not want our people to listen and understand the solution that God has given the Honorable Elijah Muhammad. The government is against Mr. Muhammad because the government is against our God. In order to trick our people away from God's true solutions, the government is trying to deceive our people with a false solution, a phony solution, a deceitful solution called token integration. I may add, whenever you get on the bus or the subway or the streetcar and you have to use a token, that token is not the real thing but it is a substitute for the real thing. And wherever you have a token, you have a substitute. And wherever you have token integration, you don't have anything but a substitute for integration and there's no real integration anywhere in North America—North, South, East, or West, not even in San Francisco, Oakland, or Berkeley.

Has the government effort to bribe our people with token integration made our plight better, or has it made it worse? When you tried to integrate the white community in search of better housing, the whites there fled to the suburbs. And the community that you thought would be integrated soon deteriorated into another all-Black slum. What happened to the liberal whites? Why did they flee? We thought that they were supposed to be our friends. And why did the neighborhood deteriorate only after our people moved in?

It is the tricky real estate agents posing as white liberal friends who encourage our people to force their way into white communities, and then they themselves sell these integrated houses at such high prices that our people again are forced to take in roomers to offset the high house notes. This creates in the new area the same overcrowded conditions, and the new community soon deteriorates into the same slum conditions from which we thought we had escaped. The only one who has benefited is the white real estate agent who poses as our friend, as a liberal, and who sells us the house in a community destined by his own greedy schemes to become nothing but a high-priced slum area.

Today our people can see that integrated housing has not solved our problems. At best it was only a temporary solution. One in which only the wealthy, handpicked Negroes found temporary benefit.

After the 1954 Supreme Court desegregation decision, the same thing happened when our people tried to integrate the schools. All the white students disappeared into the suburbs. Now the caliber of what our people thought was to be an integrated school has fallen to the same level of the slum school from which we thought we had escaped. Just as efforts to integrate housing failed miserably, efforts to integrate schools have been an even more miserable failure.

Having failed to get integrated housing and failed to get integrated schools, now the Negro leaders are demanding integrated jobs. That is they are demanding a certain quota, or percentage, of white people's jobs.

Violence and Bloodshed

First the Negro leadership demanded the white man's house, and the whites vacated their run-down houses for us and built new homes for themselves out in the suburbs. Then the Negro leaders demanded seats for our children in the white man's schools. The whites evacuated the schools as our children moved in and they built modern schools for themselves in the suburbs. But now the Negro leadership is demanding the white man's job. Can the whites vacate their jobs like they did their homes and their schools and move to the suburbs and create more jobs? No. Not without violence and bloodshed. The same white liberals who used to praise our people for their patient nonviolent approach have now become openly impatient and violent themselves in defense of their own jobs. Not only in the South but also in the North. Even here in the Bay Area.

For thirty-three years the Honorable Elijah Muhammad has been warning us that the time would come when the white man would not have enough jobs for himself much less enough jobs for our people. So the present demand of our people for more of the white man's jobs must lead to violence and bloodshed. It may even lead to a race war—a bloody race war. And it is the government itself that is now pressing the people of this country into a racial bloodbath.

But the white man is misjudging the times and he is underestimating the American so-called Negro because we're living in a new day. Our people are now a new people. That old Uncle Tom–type Negro is dead. Our people have no more fear of anyone, no more fear of anything. We are not afraid to go to jail. We are not afraid to give our very life itself. And we're not afraid to take the lives of those who try to take our lives. We believe in a fair exchange.

We believe in a fair exchange. An eye for an eye. A tooth for a tooth. A head for a head and life for a life. If this is the price of freedom, we won't hesitate to pay the price.

By trying to oppose the divine solution that God has given to the Honorable Elijah Muhammad, the American government will actually provoke another Civil War. That is, this government—and especially that present administration in Washington, D.C.—will provoke a civil war among whites by trying to force them to give up their jobs and homes and schools to our people. And our people will provoke a race war by trying to take the white man's jobs and his schools and his home away from him.

This racial dilemma poses a serious problem for white America. Civil war between whites on the one hand, a race war between the whites and their 20 million ex-slaves on the other hand. And the entire dark world is watching, waiting to see what the American government will do to solve this problem once and for all.

We must have a permanent solution. A temporary solution won't do. Tokenism will no longer suffice. The Honorable Elijah Muhammad has the only permanent solution. Twenty million ex-slaves must be permanently separated from our former slavemaster and placed on some land that we can call our own. Then we can create our own jobs. Control our own economy. Solve our own problems instead of waiting on the American white man to solve our problems for us.

The Honorable Elijah Muhammad teaches us that on our own land we can set up farms, factories, businesses. We can establish our own government and become an independent nation. And once we become separated from the jurisdiction of this white nation, we can then enter into trade and commerce for ourselves with other independent nations. This is the only solution.

The Honorable Elijah Muhammad says that in our own land we can establish our own agricultural system. We can grow food to feed our own people. We can raise cattle and use the hides, the leather, and the wool to clothe our people. We can dig the clay from the earth and make bricks to build homes for our people. We can turn the trees into lumber and furnish the homes for our own people.

He says that we can dig the natural resources from the earth once we are in our own land. Land is the basis of all economic security. Land is essential to freedom, justice, and equality. Land is essential to true independence. And the Honorable Elijah Muhammad says we must be separated from the American white man, returned to our own land where we can live among our own people. This is the only true solution.

For just as the biblical government of Egypt under Pharaoh was against Moses because Moses had been directed by God to separate the Hebrew slaves from Pharaoh and lead them out of the house of bondage to a land of their own, today this modern house of bondage under the authority of the American government opposes this modern Moses. Opposes the Honorable Elijah Muhammad's efforts to separate our people, who have been made slaves here in this country, and lead us to a land of our own.

The government opposes the Honorable Elijah Muhammad's efforts to wake us up, clean us up, and stand us on our own feet so we can follow him out of this house of bondage to our own land where we can live among our own people. Just as the government of biblical Egypt was against the God of the Hebrew slaves, today the American government is against the

God of her Negro slaves, the God of our forefathers. And just as that Pharaoh tried to trick the Hebrew slaves into rejecting the offers of salvation from their God by deceiving them with false promises through hired magicians and carefully staged demonstrations like the recent ridiculous march on Washington [the 1963 civil rights march that drew more than 250,000 people for an August 28 rally at the Lincoln Memorial], today this government is paying certain elements of the Negro leadership to deceive our people into thinking that we're going to get accepted soon into the mainstream of American life.

The government is deceiving our people with false promises so we won't want to return to our own land and people. The government is saying, "Stay here, don't listen to this Muhammad, we will desegregate the lunch counters and the theaters and the parks and the toilets"—meaning this public accommodation thing where you can sit on a toilet with a white person or in a toilet with a white person.

"We'll give you more civil rights bills. We won't give you civil rights, but we'll give you civil rights bills." The government promises our people this only to keep you from listening to the Honorable Elijah Muhammad and to stop us from waking up. They know that if we listen to the Honorable Elijah Muhammad long enough, we will begin to do our own thinking. He'll make us see, hear, think, and able to speak for ourselves.

Whenever you become fed up in this country with the white man's brutality and you get set to take matters in your own hands in order to defend yourself and your people, the same government—and again I repeat, especially that Catholic administration in Washington, D.C.—tries to pacify our people with deceitful promises of tricky civil rights legislation that is never designed to be a true solution to our problem. Civil rights legislation will never solve our problems. The white liberals are nothing but political hypocrites who use our people as political footballs only to get bills passed that will increase their own power.

The present proposed civil rights legislation will give the present administration dictatorial powers and make America a legal police state, but still won't solve the race problem. The present administration is only using civil rights as a political football to gain more legislation and power for itself. Our people are being used as pawns in the game of power politics by political hypocrites. They don't want our people to listen to the Honorable Elijah Muhammad because they know he will make them—make us see them as they really are.

American Propaganda

So I say in my conclusion, the Honorable Elijah Muhammad's message and solution is simple. He says: "Since we are not wanted in this country, let's pack our bags and go back home to our own people, to our own land." The propaganda of the American government is skillfully designed to make our people think that our people back home don't want us. Government propagandists tell us constantly, "Africa is a jungle. Africans are savage and backward. They have no modern conveniences and you're too much like us white folks. How could you live comfortably back there?"

This propaganda is government strategy against the Honorable Elijah Muhammad, realizing that his mission is to teach our people the truth about our own kind, clean us up, and then return us to our own land and unite us with our own people. The American government turns us against our own kind in order to keep us from making a mass exodus out of this country where we can live at home among our own people.

Therefore, the Honorable Elijah Muhammad says, American propaganda is designed to make us think that no matter how much hell we catch here, we're still better off in America than we'd be anywhere else. They want us to think we have no place else to go. And many of our so-called intellectuals who pose as our leaders and spokesmen actually believe that we have no place else to go. So their solution to our problem is that we stay here and continue to catch hell from the American white man.

But the only permanent solution is complete separation or some land of our own in a country of our own. All other courses will lead to violence and bloodshed. It will lead to the destruction of America, and it will also lead to the destruction of our people who fall for it. So his message is flee for your lives and save yourselves. And I thank you.

I Have a Dream

Martin Luther King Jr.

The Reverend Martin Luther King Jr. gained national prominence in 1955 when he organized a boycott to protest Montgomery's segregated bus system—a move that ultimately ended segregation in public transportation. Until his death in 1968, King continued to work tirelessly for black rights, inspiring peaceful sit-ins at segregated restaurants and organizing myriad demonstrations in his systematic attack on segregation and other racial inequities. Above all, King's unwavering dedication to nonviolent resistance as a weapon in the struggle for justice and freedom shaped the entire civil rights movement.

In 1963 civil rights leaders began planning a dramatic action—the March on Washington. This landmark civil rights demonstration brought over 250,000 people—both black and white—together before the Lincoln Memorial in Washington, D.C. King was asked to deliver the keynote address. Always a persuasive speaker, King electrified the huge crowd—and the entire nation via television—when he spoke the unforgettable words that so eloquently defined the goals of the civil rights movement: "I have a dream that my four little children will one day live in a nation where they will not be judged by the color of their skin but by the content of their character." King's address, perhaps his most well known, is reprinted here.

I am happy to join with you today in what will go down in history as the greatest demonstration for freedom in the history of our nation.

Five score years ago, a great American, in whose symbolic shadow we stand today, signed the Emancipation Proclamation. This momentous decree came as a great beacon light of hope to millions of Negro slaves who had been seared in the flames of withering injustice. It came as a joyous daybreak to end the long night of their captivity.

But 100 years later, the Negro still is not free. One hundred years later, the life of the Negro is still sadly crippled by the manacles of segregation and the chains of discrimination. One hundred years later, the Negro lives on a lonely island of poverty in the midst of a vast ocean of material prosperity. One hundred years later, the Negro is still languished in the corners of American society and finds himself an exile in his own land. And so we've come here today to dramatize a shameful condition.

Unalienable Rights

In a sense we've come to our nation's capital to cash a check. When the architects of our republic wrote the magnificent words of the Constitution and the Declaration of Independence, they were signing a promissory note to which every American was to fall heir. This note was a promise that all men—yes, black men as well as white men—would be guaranteed the unalienable rights of life, liberty, and the pursuit of happiness.

It is obvious today that America has defaulted on this promissory note insofar as her citizens of color are concerned. Instead of honoring this sacred obligation, America has given the Negro people a bad check, a check that has come back marked "insufficient funds."

But we refuse to believe that the bank of justice is bankrupt. We refuse to believe that there are insufficient funds in the great vaults of opportunity of this nation. And so we've come to cash this check, a check that will give us upon demand the riches of freedom and security of justice. We have also come to his hallowed spot to remind America of the fierce urgency of *now*. This is no time to engage in the luxury of cooling off or to take the tranquilizing drug of gradualism. Now is the time to make real the promises of democracy. Now is the time to rise from the dark and desolate valley of segregation to the sunlit path of racial justice. Now is the time to lift our nation from the quicksands of racial injustice to the solid rock of brotherhood. Now is the time to make justice a reality for all of God's children.

It would be fatal for the nation to overlook the urgency of the moment. This sweltering summer of the Negro's legitimate discontent will not pass until there is an invigorating autumn of freedom and equality. Nineteen sixty-three is not an end but a beginning. Those who hoped that the Negro needed to blow off steam and will now be content will have a rude awakening if the nation returns to business as usual. There will be neither rest nor tranquility in America until the Negro is granted his citizenship rights. The whirlwinds of revolt will continue to shake the foundations of our nation until the bright day of justice emerges.

But there is something that I must say to my people who stand on the warm threshold which leads into the palace of justice. In the process of gaining our rightful place we must not be guilty of wrongful deeds. Let us not seek to satisfy our thirst for freedom by drinking from the cup of bitterness and hatred. We must forever conduct our struggle on the high

Participants walk in the 1963 March on Washington, where over 250,000 people gathered at the Lincoln Memorial in Washington, D.C.

plane of dignity and discipline. We must not allow our creative protest to degenerate into physical violence. Again and again we must rise to the majestic heights of meeting physical force with soul force. The marvelous new militancy which has engulfed the Negro community must not lead us to a distrust of all white people, for many of our white brothers, as evidenced by their presence here today, have come to realize that their destiny is tied up with our destiny. And they have come to realize that their freedom is inextricably bound to our freedom. We cannot walk alone.

The Long March Ahead

And as we walk, we must make the pledge that we shall always march ahead. We cannot turn back. There are those who are asking the devotees of civil rights, "When will you be satisfied?" We can never be satisfied as long as the Negro is the victim of the unspeakable horrors of police brutality. We can never be satisfied as long as our bodies, heavy with the fatigue of travel, cannot gain lodging in the motels of the highways and the hotels of the cities. We cannot be satisfied as long as the Negro's basic mobility is from a smaller ghetto to a larger one. We can never be satisfied as long as our children are stripped of their selfhood and robbed of their dignity by signs stating "for whites only." We cannot be satisfied as long as a Negro in Mississippi cannot vote and a Negro in New York believes he has nothing for which to vote. No, no we are not satisfied and we will not be satisfied until justice rolls down like waters and righteousness like a mighty stream.

I am not unmindful that some of you have come here out of great trials and tribulations. Some of you have come fresh from narrow jail cells. Some of you have come from areas where your quest for freedom left you battered by storms of persecution and staggered by the winds of police brutality. You have been the veterans of creative suffering. Continue to work with the faith that unearned suffering is redemptive.

Go back to Mississippi, go back to Alabama, go back to South Carolina, go back to Georgia, go back to Louisiana, go back to the slums and ghettos of our northern cities, knowing that somehow this situation can and will be changed.

I Have a Dream

Let us not wallow in the valley of despair. I say to you today my friends—so even though we face the difficulties of today and tomorrow, I still have a dream. It is a dream deeply rooted in the American dream.

I have a dream that one day this nation will rise up and live out the true meaning of its creed: "We hold these truths to be self-evident, that all men are created equal."

I have a dream that one day on the red hills of Georgia the sons of former slaves and the sons of former slave owners will be able to sit down together at the table of brotherhood.

I have a dream that one day even the state of Mississippi, a state sweltering with the heat of injustice, sweltering with the heat of oppression, will be transformed into an oasis of freedom and justice.

I have a dream that my four little children will one day live in a nation where they will not be judged by the color of their skin but by the content of their character.

I have a dream today.

I have a dream that one day down in Alabama, with its vicious racists, with its governor having his lips dripping with the words of interposition and nullification—one day right there in Alabama little black boys and black girls will be able to join hands with little white boys and white girls as sisters and brothers.

I have a dream today.

I have a dream that one day every valley shall be exalted, and every hill and mountain shall be made low, the rough places will be made plain, and the crooked places will be made straight, and the glory of the Lord shall be revealed and all flesh shall see it together.

This is our hope. This is the faith that I go back to the South with. With this faith we will be able to hew out of the mountain of despair a stone of hope. With this faith we will be able to transform the jangling discords of our nation into a beautiful symphony of brotherhood. With this faith we will be able to work together, to pray together, to struggle together, to go to jail together, to stand up for freedom together, knowing that we will be free one day.

This will be the day, this will be the day when all of God's children will be able to sing with new meaning "My country 'tis of thee, sweet land of liberty, of thee I sing. Land where my father's died, land of the Pilgrim's pride, from every mountainside, let freedom ring!"

Let Freedom Ring

And if America is to be a great nation, this must become true. And so let freedom ring from the prodigious hilltops of New Hampshire. Let freedom ring from the mighty mountains of New York. Let freedom ring from the heightening Alleghenies of Pennsylvania.

Let freedom ring from the snow-capped Rockies of Colorado. Let freedom ring from the curvaceous slopes of California.

But not only that; let freedom ring from Stone Mountain of Georgia.

Let freedom ring from Lookout Mountain of Tennessee.

Let freedom ring from every hill and molehill of Mississippi—from every mountainside.

Let freedom ring. And when this happens, and when we allow freedom ring—when we let it ring from every village and every hamlet, from every state and every city, we will be able to speed up that day when all of God's children—black men and white men, Jews and Gentiles, Protestants and Catholics—will be able to join hands and sing in the words of the old Negro spiritual: "Free at last! Free at last! Thank God Almighty, we are free at last!"

Segregation Now, Segregation Forever

George Wallace

As the campaign for civil rights gained momentum in the early sixties, a host of southern white leaders, including Arkansas governor Orval Faubus, Mississippi governor Ross Barnett, and Alabama sheriff Bull Connor, gained notoriety for their white supremacist views—and their brazen efforts to thwart the progress of blacks. In this political climate, Alabama governor George Wallace stood out not only as an ardent segregationist, but also as an outspoken critic of the federal government. In his 1962 gubernatorial campaign, for instance, Wallace appealed to white southerners with promises, in part, to defy court-ordered integration and keep segregation intact throughout Alabama schools; Wallace won the race by a margin unprecedented in Alabama history. In his inaugural address in January 1963, excerpted here, Wallace reiterated his stance: "I draw the line in the dust and toss the gauntlet before the feet of tyranny . . . and I say . . . segregation now . . . segregation tomorrow . . . segregation forever."

Wallace had the opportunity to make good his promises less than six months later, when a federal judge ordered the University of Alabama to admit two black students. In a dramatic confrontation, Wallace stood at the schoolhouse door to personally block the students' entrance, yielding only when the federalized Alabama National Guard arrived.

Excerpted from George Wallace's inaugural address, January 14, 1963.

Today I have stood, where once Jefferson Davis stood, and took an oath to my people. It is very appropriate then that from this Cradle of the Confederacy, this very Heart of the Great Anglo-Saxon Southland, that today we sound the drum for freedom as have our generations of forebears before us done, time and time again through history. Let us rise to the call of freedom-loving blood that is in us and send our answer to the tyranny that clanks its chains upon the South. In the name of the greatest people that have ever trod this earth, I draw the line in the dust and toss the gauntlet before the feet of tyranny . . . and I say . . . segregation today . . . segregation tomorrow . . . segregation forever.

The Washington, D.C., school riot report is disgusting and revealing. We will not sacrifice our children to any such type school system—and you can write that down. The federal troops in Mississippi could be better used guarding the safety of the citizens of Washington, D.C., where it is even unsafe to walk or go to a ballgame—and that is the nation's capitol. I was safer in a B-29 bomber over Japan during the war in an air raid, than the people of Washington are walking to the White House neighborhood. A closer example is Atlanta. The city officials fawn for political reasons over school integration and THEN build barricades to stop residential integration—what hypocrisy!

A Message to Washington

Let us send this message back to Washington by our representatives who are with us today . . . that from this day we are standing up, and the heel of tyranny does not fit the neck of an upright man . . . that we intend to take the offensive and carry our fight for freedom across the nation, wielding the balance of power we know we possess in the Southland . . . that WE, not the insipid bloc of voters of some sections . . . will determine in the next election who shall sit in the White House of these United States. . . . That from this day, from this hour . . . from this minute . . . we give the word of a race of honor that we will tolerate their boot in our face no longer . . . and let those certain judges put that in their opium pipes of power and smoke it for what it is worth.

Hear me, Southerners! You sons and daughters who have moved north and west throughout this nation. . . . We call on you from your native soil to join with us in national support and vote . . . and we know . . . wherever you are . . . away from the hearths of the Southland . . . that you will respond, for though you may live in the fartherest reaches of this vast country . . . your heart has never left Dixieland.

And you native sons and daughters of old New England's rock-ribbed patriotism . . . and you sturdy natives of the great Mid-West . . . and you descendants of the far West flaming spirit of pioneer freedom . . . we invite you to come and be with us . . . for you are of the Southern spirit . . . and the Southern philosophy . . . you are Southerners too and brothers with us in our fight.

What I have said about segregation goes double this day . . . and what I have said to or about some federal judges goes TRIPLE this day. . . .

To realize our ambitions and to bring to fruition our dreams, we as Alabamians must take cognizance of the world about us. We must re-define our heritage, re-school our thoughts in the lessons our forefathers knew so well, first hand, in order to function and to grow and to prosper. We can no longer hide our head in the sand and tell ourselves that the ideology of our free fathers is not being attacked and is not being threatened by another idea . . . for it is. We are faced with an idea that if a centralized government assumes enough authority, enough power over its people, that it can provide a utopian life . . . that if given the power to dictate, to forbid, to require, to demand, to distribute, to edict and to judge what is best and enforce that will produce only "good" . . . and it shall be our father . . . and our God. . . .

An Ungodly Government

We find we have replaced faith with fear . . . and though we may give lip service to the Almighty . . . in reality, government has become our god. It is, therefore, a basically ungodly government and its appeal to the pseudo-intellectual and the politician is to change their status from servant of the people to master of the people . . . to play at being God . . . without faith in God . . . and without the wisdom of God. It is a system that is the very opposite of Christ for it feeds and encourages everything degenerate and base in our people as it assumes the responsibilities that we ourselves should assume. Its pseudo-liberal spokesmen and some Harvard advocates have never examined the logic of its substitution of what it calls "human rights" for individual rights, for its propaganda play on words has appeal for the unthinking. Its logic is totally material and irresponsible as it runs the full gamut of human desires . . . including the theory that everyone has voting rights without the spiritual responsibility of preserving freedom. Our founding fathers recognized those rights . . . but only within the framework of those spiritual responsibilities. But the strong, simple faith and sane reasoning of our founding fathers has long since been forgotten as the so-called "progressives" tell us that our Constitution was written for "horse and buggy" days . . . so were the Ten Commandments.

Not so long ago men stood in marvel and awe at the cities, the buildings, the schools, the autobahns that the government of Hitler's Germany had built . . . just as centuries before they stood in wonder of Rome's buildings . . . but it could not stand . . . for the system that built it had rotted the souls of the builders . . . and in turn . . . rotted the founda-

Governor George Wallace stands in the doorway at the University of Alabama, in an attempt to block the admission of two black students.

tion of what God meant that men should be. Today that same system on an international scale is sweeping the world. It is the "changing world" of which we are told . . . it is called "new" and "liberal." It is as old as the oldest dictator. It is degenerate and decadent. As the national racism of Hitler's Germany persecuted a national minority to the whim of a national majority . . . so the international racism of the liberals seek to persecute the international white minority to the whim of the international colored majority . . . so that we are footballed about according to the favor of the Afro-Asian bloc. But the Belgian survivors of the Congo cannot present their case to a war crimes commission . . . nor the Portuguese of Angola . . . nor the survivors of Castro . . . nor the citizens of Oxford, Mississippi.

It is this theory of international power politic that led a group of men on the Supreme Court for the first time in American history to issue an edict, based not on legal precedent, but upon a volume, the editor of which said our Constitution is outdated and must be changed and the writers of which, some had admittedly belonged to as many as half a hundred communist-front organizations. It is this theory that led this same group of men to briefly bare the ungodly core of that philosophy in forbidding little school children to say a prayer. And we find the evidence of that ungodliness even in the removal of the words "in God we trust" from some of our dollars, which was placed there as like evidence by our founding fathers as the faith upon which this system of government was built. It is the spirit of power thirst that caused a President in Washington to take up Caesar's pen and with one stroke of it make a law. A law which the law making body of Congress refused to pass . . . a law that tells us that we can or cannot buy or sell our very homes, except by his conditions . . . and except at HIS discretion. It is the spirit of power thirst that led the same President to launch a full offensive of twenty-five thousand troops against a university . . . of all places . . . in his own country . . . and against his own people, when this nation maintains only six thousand troops in the beleaguered city of Berlin. We have witnessed such acts of "might makes right" over the world as men yielded to the temptation to play God . . . but we have never before witnessed it in America. We reject such acts as free men. We do not defy, for there is nothing to defy . . . since as free men we do not recognize any government right to give freedom . . . or deny freedom. No government erected by man has that right. As Thomas Jefferson said, "The God who gave us life, gave us liberty at the same time; no King holds the right of liberty in his hands." Nor does any ruler in American government. . . .

United of the Many

This nation was never meant to be a unit of one . . . but a united of the many. . . . That is the exact reason our freedom loving forefathers established the states, so as to divide the rights and powers among the states, insuring that no central power could gain master government control.

In united effort we were meant to live under this government . . . whether Baptist, Methodist, Presbyterian, Church of Christ, or whatever one's denomination or religious belief . . . each respecting the other's right to a separate denomination . . . each, by working to develop his own, enriching the total of all our lives through united effort. And so it was meant in our political lives . . . whether Republican, Democrat, Prohibition, or whatever political party . . . each striving from his separate political station . . . respecting the rights of others to be separate and work from within their political framework . . . and each separate political station making its contribution to our lives. . . .

And so it was meant in our racial lives . . . each race, within its own framework has the freedom to teach . . . to instruct . . . to develop . . . to ask for and receive deserved help from others of separate racial stations. This is the great freedom of our American founding fathers . . . but if we amalgamate into the one unit as advocated by the communist philosophers . . . then the enrichment of our lives . . . the freedom for our development . . . is gone forever. We become, therefore, a mongrel unit of one under a single all powerful government . . . and we stand for everything . . . and for nothing.

The true brotherhood of America, of respecting the separateness of others . . . and uniting in effort . . . has been so twisted and distorted from its original concept that there is a small wonder that communism is winning the world.

We invite the negro citizens of Alabama to work with us from his separate racial station . . . as we will work with him . . . to develop, to grow in individual freedom and enrichment. We want jobs and a good future for BOTH races . . . the tubercular and the infirm. This is the basic heritage of my religion, of which I make full practice . . . for we are all the handiwork of God.

But we warn those, of any group, who would follow the false doctrine of communistic amalgamation that we will not surrender our system of government . . . our freedom of race and religion . . . that freedom was won at a hard price and if it requires a hard price to retain it . . . we are able . . . and quite willing to pay it.

The liberals' theory that poverty, discrimination and lack of opportunity is the cause of communism is a false theory . . . if it were true the South would have been the biggest single communist bloc in the western hemisphere long ago . . . for after the great War Between the States, our people faced a desolate land of burned universities, destroyed crops and homes, with manpower depleted and crippled, and even the mule, which was required to work the land, was so scarce that whole communities shared one animal to make the spring plowing. There were no government handouts, no Marshall Plan aid, no coddling to make sure that our people would not suffer; instead the South was set upon by the vulturous carpetbagger and federal troops, all loyal Southerners were denied the vote at the point of bayonet, so that the infamous, illegal 14th Amendment might be passed. There was no money, no food and no hope of either. But our grandfathers bent their knee only in church and bowed their head only to God. . . .

Southerners played a most magnificent part in erecting this great divinely inspired system of freedom . . . and as God is our witness, Southerners will save it.

Let us, as Alabamians, grasp the hand of destiny and walk out of the shadow of fear . . . and fill our divine destination. Let us not simply defend . . . but let us assume the leadership of the fight and carry our leadership across this nation. God has placed us here in this crisis . . . let us not fail in this . . . our most historical moment.

Voting Rights

Fannie Lou Hamer

Though poor, uneducated, and lesser known than many civil rights leaders of her day, the incorrigible Fannie Lou Hamer was at the forefront of the struggle for black rights. Despite humble beginnings—she was born to impoverished sharecroppers and never finished high school—Hamer became politically active when, in 1962, she attended what was to be her first of many civil rights rallies. At the time, many civil rights leaders were embroiled in challenging unjust voting laws and practices— the poll taxes, literacy tests, economic reprisals, intimidation, and harassment that prevented most blacks from voting. The Student Nonviolent Coordinating Committee (SNCC), for example, had recently launched a major black voter registration drive. After attending one such SNCC meeting, Hamer became compelled to act: On August 31, 1962, Hamer and a group of her peers boarded a bus bound for a county courthouse in Mississippi, where the group would attempt to register to vote.

What transpired is the subject of the following speech, delivered by Hamer at the 1964 Democratic National Convention. In a moving plea for fair voting rights, Hamer relates what she was forced to endure—she was savagely beaten and fired from her job—simply for exercising her constitutional right to vote.

Mr. Chairman, and the Credentials Committee, my name is Mrs. Fannie Lou Hamer, and I live at 626 East Lafayette Street, Ruleville, Mississippi, Sun-

Excerpted from Fannie Lou Hamer's speech to the Credentials Committee of the Democratic National Convention, Atlantic City, New Jersey, August 22, 1964.

flower County, the home of Senator James O. Eastland, and Senator John C. Stennis.

It was the 31st of August in 1962 that eighteen of us traveled twenty-six miles to the county courthouse in Indianola to try to register to try to become first-class citizens.

We was met in Indianola by Mississippi men, Highway Patrolmens, and they only allowed two of us in to take the literacy test at the time. After we had taken this test and started back to Ruleville, we was held up by the City Police and the State Highway Patrolmen and carried back to Indianola where the bus driver was charged that day with driving a bus the wrong color.

After we paid the fine among us, we continued on to Ruleville, and Reverend Jeff Sunny carried me four miles in the rural area where I had worked as a timekeeper and sharecropper for eighteen years. I was met there by my children, who told me the plantation owner was angry because I had gone down to try to register.

After they told me, my husband came, and said the plantation owner was raising Cain because I had tried to register, and before he quit talking the plantation owner came, and said, "Fannie Lou, do you know—did Pap tell you what I said?"

And I said, "Yes, sir."

He said, "I mean that," he said, "If you don't go down and withdraw your registration, you will have to leave," he said, "Then if you go down and withdraw," he said, "You will—you might have to go because we're not ready for that in Mississippi."

And I addressed him and told him and said, "I didn't try to register for you. I tried to register for myself."

I had to leave that same night.

On the 10th of September, 1962, sixteen bullets was fired into the home of Mr. and Mrs. Robert Tucker for me. That same night two girls were shot in Ruleville, Mississippi. Also Mr. Joe McDonald's house was shot in.

And in June, the 9th, 1963, I had attended a voter registration workshop, was returning back to Mississippi. Ten of us was traveling by the Continental Trailway bus. When we got to Winona, Mississippi, which is Montgomery County, four of the people got off to use the washroom, and two of the people—to use the restaurant—two of the people wanted to use the washroom.

The four people that had gone in to use the restaurant was ordered out. During this time I was on the bus. But when I looked through the window and saw they had rushed out I got off of the bus to see what had happened, and one of the ladies said, "It was a State Highway Patrolman and a Chief of Police ordered us out."

I got back on the bus and one of the persons [who] had used the washroom got back on the bus, too.

As soon as I was seated on the bus, I saw when they began to get the four people in a highway patrolman's car, [so] I stepped off of the bus to see what was happening and somebody screamed from the car that the four workers was in and said, "Get that one there," and when I went to get in the car, when the man told me I was under arrest, he kicked me.

I was carried to the county jail, and put in the booking room. They left some of the people in the booking room and began to place us in cells. I was placed in a cell with a young woman called Miss Ivesta Simpson. After I was placed in the cell I began to hear sounds of licks and screams. I could hear the sounds of licks and horrible screams, and I could hear somebody say, "Can you say, 'Yes, sir,' nigger?" Can you say, 'Yes, sir?'"

And they would say other horrible names.

She would say, "Yes, I can say, 'Yes, sir.'"

"So, say it."

She says, "I don't know you well enough."

They beat her, I don't know how long, and after a while she began to pray, and asked God to have mercy on those people.

And it wasn't too long before three white men came to my cell. One of these men was a State Highway Patrolman and he asked me where I was from, and I told him Ruleville, [and] he said, "We are going to check this."

And they left my cell and it wasn't too long before they came back. He said, "You are from Ruleville all right," and he used a curse word, and he said, "We are going to make you wish you was dead."

A Savage Beating

I was carried out of that cell into another cell where they had two Negro prisoners. The State Highway Patrolmen ordered the first Negro to take the blackjack.

The first Negro prisoner ordered me, by orders from the State Highway Patrolman for me, to lay down on a bunk bed on my face, and I laid on my face.

The first Negro began to beat, and I was beat by the first Negro until he was exhausted, and I was holding my hands behind me at that time on my left side because I suffered from polio when I was six years old.

After the first Negro had beat until he was exhausted the State Highway Patrolman ordered the second Negro to take the blackjack. The second Negro began to beat and I began to work my feet, and the State Highway Patrolman ordered the first Negro who had beat to set on my feet to keep me from working my feet. I began to scream and one white man got up and began to beat me in my head and tell me to hush.

One white man—my dress had worked up high, he walked over and pulled my dress down and he pulled my dress back, back up.

I was in jail when Medgar Evers was murdered.

All of this is on account we want to register, to become first-class citizens, and if the Freedom Democratic Party is not seated now, I question America, is this America, the land of the free and the home of the brave where we have to sleep with our telephones off of the hooks because our lives be threatened daily because we want to live as decent human beings, in America?

Thank you.

Black Pride

James Farmer

James Farmer helped found the Congress of Racial
Equality (CORE), a group dedicated to fighting racial injustice. As national director of CORE, Farmer steered the
organization toward nonviolent protest as a means of
breaking down racial barriers. Many of the programs
that Farmer initiated—sit-ins, boycotts, and Freedom
Rides, for example—focused on ending segregation in
public facilities. Throughout his distinguished career,
Farmer remained a steadfast proponent of integration
over separation, although he did over time move away
from his pacifist convictions.

In the following address delivered at Lincoln University in 1967, Farmer explains why the black community
is dissatisfied with the progress of the civil rights movement, asserting that "there has been no substantial
change in the plight or the position of the black man."

I f our movement these past years has been a revolution, as
it has been called, then we are forced to say that the revolution has failed. We are forced to say that the victories
have not yet been meaningful to the masses of people, and
this is precisely the present dilemma of the movement now,
and the present crisis.

I spend a lot of time—too much time—traveling around
the country. I sort of feel the pulse of the segment of the Negro community that I come in contact with, and the white
community. The impression I get is that we are now indeed
in an area of pessimism in the whole movement. And the pessimism, indeed, has some basis and reality. We have won vic-

Excerpted from James Farmer's speech at Lincoln University, Pennsylvania, February 25, 1967.

tories. One cannot travel through the South without seeing those victories—in voting rights, in public places.

I was in Little Rock, Arkansas, not too long ago. I stopped a Negro on the street and asked him if things had changed there greatly, over the last few years. The last time I was in the city, about ten years ago, there were screaming mobs in the streets as those children were trying to get into Central High. He looked me in the face and said: "Brother Farmer, everything has changed, but everything remains the same. Yes, I can now buy a hot dog at that lunch counter. Big deal." Somehow that hot dog doesn't seem nearly so important as it did a few years ago.

A footnote here: I think that this is one of the problems with which we must deal. The fact that a little progress like a hot dog does not satisfy the appetite. It merely whets the appetite. Although, I think that this is of such stuff that further progress is made.

But my friend went on talking. He said: "Yes, I can go downtown and check into a hotel, if I had the money, which I don't. I have been out of work for six months. And furthermore, if I go three miles outside the city, I won't know that there ever was a Civil Rights Act of 1964. And yes, we can sit on the front seat of a bus. We can go to the theater and sit in the audience; we can buy a hot dog and a hamburger. Everything has changed but everything remains the same."

The Age of Pessimism

And I think it has, essentially. There has been no substantial change in the plight or the position of the black man in our country. And that is why the age of pessimism has come upon the movement. And that is why the "little people" in the ghetto community feel so completely frustrated and left out. As Richard Wright put it in one of his novels: "Sometimes I feel like I am on the outside of the world looking in through a knothole in the fence." And I think that this is the feeling among the people in the ghetto who, literally, have not been substantially relieved by our battle.

In 1942, when there was no real movement of CORE, we had a small band of young idealists, mostly college students, who had been studying Gandhi, his programs and methods, and had come to the conclusion that his techniques of non-violence really worked. And they used them in those days, for sitting-in, waiting-in, et cetera, and nonviolence became, for a long time, the watchword for a large segment of the movement. Now nonviolence is under considerable fire. And to a great extent, I would say that it is repudiated by the masses of people in the ghetto, essentially because the movement has not yet won victories which have changed their life situations. They live in the same tenement slums, in the Northern cities; in the rural areas of the South, in the same sharecropper–tenant-farmer shacks, and they are equally unemployed. This is as they were a few years ago before the movement got started.

Then what have we accomplished? Nothing? By no means. We have succeeded in elevating life for those of us who are in the middle classes. We have given greater mobility to the Negro middle-class man in our society.

A Widening Economic Gap

Economically, the Negro has improved—but in absolute terms, not in relative terms. Relatively, we are becoming increasingly aware that the plot has worsened. I wouldn't go around the country as George Wallace does—he's one of the governors of Alabama—saying that our colored people have a high and rapidly rising standard of living. He says that black people have a standard of living higher than any place in Africa, as though that is any basis for comparison. The only basis for comparison is that of a Negro in the United States and one will find that the gap between the average Negro and the average white has widened since World War II.

During the war, there was a narrowing of the gap, but since the war, there has been a widening of the gap. The average income of Negroes in 1950 was 53% of the average income of whites; 1961, 52%. In spite of the fact that hundreds of thousands of Negroes have migrated from rural areas in the South to urban centers in the North and normally one would expect an improvement in the standard of living. In spite of the fact also that the educational gap had slightly closed in that period of time. One would expect that to correct itself in the closing of the income gap. That did not happen.

Segregation in our land is not decreasing, it is increasing. I said that if our struggle had been a revolution, then it is a revolution that has failed. The integration fight has not been successful. It has failed too. Residential segregation is increasing all over the country. Recently I was in various cities in the Northwest which I visited twenty years ago. I observed much more segregation there than when they had few Negroes who had been there for generations. They lived just about any place they wanted. As the Negro population increased following the war, the ghettos were established. The rigid lines were set up and Negroes were excluded from other areas. In other places in the North one finds that the old pattern of the black core and the white noose is still perpetuated and the Negro population increases and the flight to the suburbs of whites presents that pattern. This results in an increase of segregation and an increase of de facto school segregation as a result. One finds in the South that many of the Southern cities are now trying to imitate the North, and now Southern cities are seeking through urban renewal and other devices to create a de facto segregation—relocation to relocate black here and white here. In a few years they will be able to say, as our Northern cities now say, "We have no segregation here; anybody who lives in this school zone is perfectly free to go to this school; it just so happens that they are all white or all black."

Broken Promises

We have to face the stark fact that segregation is increasing, not decreasing. The anger and frustration in the ghetto community is growing. As I travel around the country, I find a greater sense of alienation than was true a few years ago. There have been so many promises and broken promises, they say. And they are right. There was a wave of optimism at the outset of the poverty program. A wave of optimism which I shared. That optimism has dissipated itself as far as the masses are concerned, it seems to me, because of the controversy, in part, of the maximum feasible participation and the fear of many of the politicians in city halls that maximum feasible participation might mean making visible those who hith-erto have been invisible, making vocal those who have been silent, and that they might indeed come to identify their plight with city hall, in a cause-and-effect relationship, and that con-troversy has continued. Today with the cutback in antipoverty funds the situation has not been improved, and on my last trip into Minnesota, the few Negroes who were there expressed to me some concern about the Civil Rights Bill which is to be in-troduced in Congress. They say what we need now is some money to get rid of the slums. I had not been aware that they had any siz-able slums in Minnesota, but they said we need to get rid of the slums and so forth, and instead we get another bill. One would not have heard such comments a few years ago. . . .

James Farmer

There is also the talk about power. The interpretation is that the power means military power and thus means violence. I think all kinds of threatening images have been conjured up in every-body's mind, and much of this is due to the press, which has strongly misinterpreted what the spokesmen have been trying to say as they speak of power. Now, I didn't choose the slogan and am not sure that I would have chosen it, but it is most important to understand the concepts that are underneath it: He is American and he is black. A few years ago I looked at the preschool books of my little girl. She had gotten quite a group of them as gifts. I wanted to see how she would see herself and what kind of image she would get. I found that in most cases she couldn't see herself at all, unless she was carrying somebody else's bag or was in some absurd position with a string tied around her toe with other kids poking fun at her and laughing. Not an acceptable image.

This occurred to me that, as we walked through the streets and looked at the billboards, she would not see herself. She would see another image. Why couldn't she identify with it? Very simply, because society has pounded into her from the very beginning of consciousness that that is not she and she is not that and thus it becomes a virtual impossibility for her to identify herself.

I think today the most aggravating struggle in the black community is this quest for identity. As [writer James] Jimmy Baldwin puts it "Who am I? Who am I? In America."

With this must go the realization in our nation that we have had such a deep split for 350 years, there is a racist aspect in our culture. One that we cannot get away from by denying, but only by facing. It is extremely difficult for any of us in our land to grow to adulthood without having at least some residual racial prejudice back of us, black or white. It takes great feats of empathy and great qualities of sensitivity for one to approach the point of overcoming it. Pick any white person at random, and probably he knows no Negroes; or perhaps only the Negro who works for him as a domestic and that is not a basis for understanding in spite of the stereotype of their being closer together and therefore understanding each other better. They actually understand each other less because of the racism that exists. Pick any Negro in the street and in all probability he knows no white people, except his boss, who pushes him around if he doesn't pull the mop fast enough; or the landlord or the merchant who exploit. And so, he develops the negative image too.

Group Pride

I say that because of this the polarization in our national community has grown so deep that now it becomes extremely difficult if not impossible for any of us to overcome it or to be free from it. And this speeds up the necessity of the black people to find identity. How do we find it? Well, by developing pride. Certainly, we need pride. We need to know more about the Negro and the contribution of the Negro to American history. We need to know more about African history and about the roots—our heritage and our tradition. That, of course, is not enough in itself. If that is all that we do, then it will be a form of intellectual masturbation. We need also to have a program to deal with the very real issue that is confronting us in the ghetto community. Pride, yes. There is nothing wrong with group pride. It only becomes bad or destructive if it becomes chauvinistic. And I oppose this.

Other groups in American history have developed pride. They have strengthened those things as they faced discrimination. I recall reading of the great wave of Irish immigration more than a century ago—at the time of the potato-crop failure in Ireland, when the Irish faced all kinds of things, signs in windows saying "Man Wanted: No Irishmen Need Apply." That sign became so widespread that they didn't have to spell it out. "Man Wanted NINA." The Irish, of course, of necessity, drew tighter together. It was inevitable. They sang songs; some bitter. One song they sang was about its being an honor to be born an Irishman. And it is. It is good. It is essential for those who are pushed around. It is an honor to be born an Irishman so long as it is not a dishonor not to be born one. In other words, so long as it doesn't become chauvinism.

I see the same thing in black identity and black pride. Let us find that pride and let us develop it and let us think of ourselves and we can answer the question what it means to be black, and from there we can find the answer to the question what it means to be an American. I don't think that we can do it the other way around. I think it has to be done in that way.

A Fully Integrated Society

Bayard Rustin

Throughout his tenure as a civil rights activist, Bayard Rustin worked for a number of pacifist organizations and helped found the Southern Christian Leadership Conference (SCLC), a national civil rights group that supported social and economic programs to spur integration. Rustin also worked closely with Martin Luther King Jr. and, in 1963, was even appointed by the famous civil rights leader to organize the March on Washington, the largest demonstration in American history up until that time.

Well known as a committed pacifist and integrationist, Rustin was often asked to speak on the issue of integration versus separatism. In 1968, at a meeting of the National Jewish Community Relations Advisory Council, Rustin participated in a debate with professor and civil rights activist Robert S. Browne, who outlined the merits of separation as a solution to racial problems. In his rebuttal, reprinted here, Rustin explains why the ideology behind the movement to separate is flawed. Rustin maintains instead that integration, in conjunction with maintaining a strong black national identity, must be the ultimate goal of the civil rights movement.

The proposition that separation may be the best solution of America's racial problems has been recurrent in American Negro history. Let us look at the syndrome that has given rise to it.

From Bayard Rustin's speech to The National Jewish Community Relations Advisory Council, 1968.

Shattered Expectations

Separation, in one form or another, has been proposed and widely discussed among American Negroes in three different periods. Each time, it was put forward in response to an identical combination of economic and social factors that induced despair among Negroes. The syndrome consists of three elements: great expectations, followed by dashed hopes, followed by despair and discussion of separation.

The first serious suggestion that Negroes should separate came in the aftermath of the Civil War. During that war many Negroes had not only been strongly in favor of freedom but had fought for the Union. It was a period of tremendous expectations. Great numbers of Negroes left the farms and followed the Union Army as General Sherman marched across Georgia to the sea; they believed that when he got to the sea they would be not only free but also given land— "forty acres and a mule." However, the compromise of 1876 and the withdrawal of the Union Army from the South dashed those expectations. Instead of forty acres and a mule all they got was a new form of slavery.

Out of the ruins of those hopes emerged Booker T. Washington, saying in essence to Negroes: "There is no hope in your attempting to vote, no hope in attempting to play any part in the political or social processes of the nation. Separate yourself from all that, and give your attention to your innards: that you are men, that you maintain dignity, that you drop your buckets where they are, that you become excellent of character."

Of course, it did not work. It could not work. Because human beings have stomachs, as well as minds and hearts, and equate dignity, first of all, not with caste, but with class. I preached the dignity of black skin color and wore my hair Afro style long before it became popular, I taught Negro history in the old Benjamin Franklin High School, where I first got my teaching experience, long before it became popular. But in spite of all that it is my conviction that there are three fundamental ways in which a group of people can maintain their dignity: one, by gradual advancement in the economic order; two, by being a participating element of the democratic process; and three, through the sense of dignity that emerges from their struggle. For instance, Negroes never had more dignity than when Martin Luther King won the boycott in Montgomery or at the bridge in Selma.

This is not to say that all the values of self-image and identification are not important and should not be stimulated; but they should be given secondary or tertiary emphasis; for, unless they rest on a sound economic and social base, they are likely only to create more frustration by raising expectation or hopes with no ability truly to follow through.

The second period of frustration and the call for separation came after World War I. During that war, 300,000 Negro troops went to France—not for the reason Mr. Wilson thought he was sending them, but because they felt that if they fought for their country they would be able to return and say: "We have fought and fought well. Now give us at home what we fought for abroad."

Again, this great expectation collapsed in total despair, as a result of postwar developments: lynchings in the United States reached their height in the early twenties; the Palmer raids did not affect Negroes directly but had such a terrifying effect on civil liberties that no one paid any attention to what was happening to Negroes; the Ku Klux Klan moved its headquarters from Georgia to Indianapolis, the heart of the so-called North; and unemployment among Negroes was higher at that period than it had ever been before. It was at that time, too, the Negroes began their great migration to the North, not from choice but because they were being driven off the land in the South by changed economic conditions.

The war having created great expectations, and the conditions following the war having shattered them, a really great movement for separation ensued—a much more significant movement than the current one. Marcus Garvey organized over two million Negroes, four times the number the NAACP has ever organized, to pay dues to buy ships to return to Africa.

Today, we are experiencing the familiar syndrome again. The Civil Rights Acts of 1964 and 1965 and the Supreme Court decisions all led people seriously to believe that progress was forthcoming, as they believed the day Martin

Luther King said, "I have a dream." What made the march on Washington in 1963 great was the fact that it was the culmination of a period of great hope and anticipation.

Despair in the Ghettos

But what has happened since? The ghettos are fuller than they have ever been, with 500,000 people moving into them each year and only some 40,000 moving out. They are the same old Bedford-Stuyvesant, Harlem, Detroit, and Watts, only they are much bigger, with more rats, more roaches, and more despair. There are more Negro youngsters in segregated schoolrooms than there were in 1954—not all due to segregation or discrimination, perhaps, but a fact. The number of youngsters who have fallen back in their reading, writing, and arithmetic since 1954 has increased, not decreased, and unemployment for Negro young women is up to 35, 40, and 50 percent in the ghettos. For young men in the ghettos, it is up to 20 percent, and this is a conservative figure. For family men, the unemployment is twice that of whites. Having built up hopes, and suffered the despair which followed, we are again in a period where separation is being discussed.

I maintain that, in all three periods, the turn to separation has been a frustration reaction to objective political, social, and economic circumstances. I believe that it is fully justified, for it would be the most egregious wishful thinking to suppose that people can be subjected to deep frustration and yet not act in a frustrated manner. But however justified and inevitable the frustration, it is totally unrealistic to divert the attention of young Negroes at this time either to the idea of a separate state in the United States, or to going back to Africa, or to setting up a black capitalism (as Mr. Nixon and CORE are now advocating), or to talk about any other possibility of economic separation, when those Negroes who are well off are the two million Negroes who are integrated into the trade union movement of this country.

This is not to belittle in any way the desirability of fostering a sense of ethnic unity or racial pride among Negroes or relationships to other black people around the world. This is all to the good, but the ability to do this in a healthy rather

than a frustrated way will depend upon the economic viabil-
ity of the Negro community, the degree to which it can participate in the democratic process here rather than separate
from it, and the degree to which it accepts methods of struggle that are productive.

I would not want to leave this subject without observing
that while social and economic conditions have precipitated
thoughts of separation, it would be an oversimplification to
attribute the present agitation of that idea exclusively to
those causes. A good deal of the talk about separation today
reflects a class problem within the Negro community.

I submit that it is not the *lumpenproletariat,* the Negro
working classes, the Negro working poor, who are proclaim-
ing: "We want Negro principals, we want Negro supervisors,
we want Negro teachers in our schools." It is the educated
Negroes. If you name a leader of that movement, you will
put your finger on a man with a master's or a Ph.D. degree.
Being blocked from moving up, he becomes not only interested in Negro children, but in getting those teaching jobs,
supervisory jobs, and principal jobs for his own economic interest. While this is understandable, it is not true that only
teachers who are of the same color can teach pupils effectively. Two teachers had an effect upon me; one was black,
and the other was white, and it was the white teacher who
had the most profound effect, not because she was white, but
because she was who she was.

Negroes have been taught that we are inferior, and many
Negroes believe that themselves, and have believed it for a
long time. That is to say, sociologically we were made children. What is now evident is that the entire black community
is rebelling against that concept in behalf of manhood and
dignity. This process of rebellion will have as many ugly
things in it as beautiful things. Like young people on the
verge of maturity many Negroes now say, "We don't want
help; we'll do it ourselves. Roll over, Whitey. If we break our
necks, okay."

Also, while rebelling, there is rejection of those who used
to be loved most. Every teenager has to go through hating
mother and father, precisely because he loves them. Now he's
got to make it on his own. Thus, [civil rights leaders] Martin

Luther King and A. Philip Randolph and Roy Wilkins and Bayard Rustin and all the people who marched in the streets are all finks now. And the liberals, and the Jews who have done most among the liberals, are also told to get the hell out of the way.

The mythology involved here can be very confusing. Jews may want now to tell their children that they lifted themselves in this society by their bootstraps. And when Negroes have made it, they will preach that ridiculous mythology too. That kind of foolishness is only good after the fact. It is not a dynamism by which the struggle can take place.

But to return to separation and nationalism. We must distinguish within this movement that which is unsound from that which is sound, for ultimately no propaganda can work for social change which is not based in absolute psychological truth.

"Reverse-ism"

There is an aspect of the present thrust toward black nationalism that I call reverse-ism. This is dangerous. Black people now want to argue that their hair is beautiful. All right. It is truthful and useful. But, to the degree that the nationalist movement takes concepts of reaction and turns them upside down and paints them glorious for no other reason than that they are black, we're in trouble—morally and politically. The Ku Klux Klan used to say: "If you're white, you're right; if you're black, no matter who you are, you're no good." And there are those among us who are now saying the opposite of the Ku Klux Klan: "He's a whitey, he's no good. Those white politicians, they both stink, don't vote for either of them. Go fishing because they're white."

The Ku Klux Klan said: "You know, we can't have black people teaching," and they put up a big fight when the first Negro was hired in a white school in North Carolina. Now, for all kinds of "glorious" reasons, we're turning that old idea upside down and saying: "Well, somehow or other, there's soul involved, and only black teachers can teach black children." But it is not true. Good teachers can teach children. The Ku Klux Klan said: "We don't want you in our community, get out." Now there are blacks saying: "We don't want any whites in our community for business or anything; get out." The Ku Klux Klan said: "We will be violent as a means of impressing our will on the situation." And now, in conference after conference a small number of black people use violence and threats to attempt to obstruct the democratic process.

Social Process

What is essential and what we must not lose sight of is that true self-respect and a true sense of image are the results of a social process and not merely a psychological state of mind.

It is utterly unrealistic to expect the Negro middle class to behave on the basis alone of color. They will behave, first of all, as middle-class people. The minute Jews got enough money to move off Allen Street, they went to West End Avenue. As soon as the Irish could get out of Hell's Kitchen, they beat it to what is now Harlem. Who thinks the Negro middle classes are going to stay in Harlem? I believe that the fundamental mistake of the nationalist movement is that it does not comprehend that class ultimately is a more driving force than color, and that any effort to build a society for American Negroes that is based on color alone is doomed to failure.

Now, there are several possibilities. One possibility is that we can stay here and continue the struggle; sometimes things will be better, sometimes they will be worse. Another is to separate ourselves into our own state in America. But I reject that because I do not believe that the American government will ever accept it. Thirdly, there is a possibility of going back to Africa, and that is out for me, because I've had enough experience with the Africans to know that they will not accept that.

Maintaining Black Identity

There is a kind of in-between position—stay here and try to separate, and yet not separate. I tend to believe that both have to go on simultaneously. That is to say there has to be a move on the part of Negroes to develop black institutions and a black image, and all this has to go on while they are going downtown into integrated work situations, while they are trying to get into the suburbs if they can, while they are doing what all other Americans do in their economic and social grasshopping. That is precisely what the Jew has done. He has held on to that which is Jewish, and nobody has made a better effort at integrating out there and making sure that he's out there where the action is. It makes for tensions, but I don't believe there's any other viable reality.

Furthermore, I believe that the most important thing for those of us in the trade union movement, in the religious communities, and in the universities is not to be taken in by methods that appeal to people's viscera but do not in fact solve the problems that stimulated their viscera.

We must fight and work for a social and economic program which will lift America's poor, whereby the Negro who is most grievously poor will be lifted to that position where he will be able to have dignity.

Secondly, we must fight vigorously for Negroes to engage in the political process, since there is only one way to have maximum feasible participation—and that is not by silly little committees deciding what they're going to do with a half million dollars, but by getting out into the real world of politics and making their weight felt. The most important thing that we have to do is to restore a sense of dignity to the Negro people. The most immediate task is for every one of us to get out and work between now and November so that we can create the kind of administration and the kind of Congress which will indeed bring about what the Freedom Budget and the Poor People's Campaign called for.

If that can happen, the intense frustration around the problem of separation will decrease as equal opportunities—economic, political, and social—increase. And that is the choice before us.

Equal Economic Opportunity

Whitney M. Young Jr.

Whitney M. Young Jr. served as dean of the School of Social Work at Atlanta University in Georgia from 1954 until 1961. Following his career in education, Young was named executive director of the National Urban League, a group founded in 1910 to expand educational and employment opportunities for blacks—preeminent goals of the civil rights movement.

In 1968 Young spoke to a group of predominantly white bank officials at the annual conference of the National Association of Bank Loan and Credit Officers. In his moving address, excerpted here, Young beseeches leaders in the business community to use their influence to provide blacks with economic opportunities—thereby giving the disenfranchised a stake in the community. Young describes why this goal is paramount not only to the black community but also to society as a whole, charging that disadvantaged blacks will lash out against a society that keeps them mired in poverty.

Only the most hopeless optimist would fail to acknowledge that our country is in deep crisis. The issues before us are several. We face a depolarization, a division between the young and the unyoung, between black and white, and between urban and rural populations. This is not a crisis that one can easily dismiss. It is one, I assure you, that is not a fad or a phenomena of a few months.

Excerpted from Whitney M. Young Jr.'s speech at the 54th Annual Fall Conference of the National Association of Bank Loan and Credit Officers, October 28, 1968.

The real situation is that the disinherited, the poor, the disadvantaged (many of whom are black in our society) are today a different breed than in the past.

They are determined, they are impatient, they are angry, and unlike the past, they are fully aware of the gap between themselves and other Americans. They are no longer concentrated in rural areas—share croppers on some isolated Southern farm where they have not the benefit of modern communication media. Today, for the most part, the disadvantaged are located in urban areas, side by side with affluence where they witness how the other half lives through their television sets or their newspapers.

They're not only aware of the difference in their status and that of other human beings, but they are also aware that that status was not God-made and God-decreed but man-made. They're not at all of a mood to assume that they are congenitally inferior but rather that they are victims of a historically selfish, callous, and sometimes brutal society. Furthermore, the disinherited today are quite aware of how other groups who felt themselves previously suppressed went about righting the wrongs and securing for themselves the advantages and the privileges and the elimination of injustice. They are aware how America rid itself of the domination of England. They are aware of how the labor movement brought about its economic freedom. They are aware of the struggles of women to get suffrage. They are aware of all of the fights of other ethnic groups and all of the techniques that they have used. And so today, they feel it is in the best American tradition to engage in similar kinds of activities that so many of us are so quick to forget. . . .

Involuntary Immigrants

Our response has also been to echo that familiar phrase, "We made it, why can't they." And there's no statement I know that's more hypocritical. The reason white people and earlier immigrants made it and black people have not made it is so simple and so clear that I find it difficult that people would even utter the phrase, "We made it, why can't they." The reason black people haven't made it is because we were the first and only involuntary immigrants to the country. For 250 years we were required to give free labor to the country as slaves during a period of time when it was illegal for us to marry and to produce families that were stable, and when it was unlawful for us to get an education. And then we have another 100 years of cheap labor because the economy then needed cheap labor.

In addition we had the added handicap of being black. We couldn't lose our identity by changing our last names like the two vice-presidential candidates, Mr. [Spiro] Agnew and Mr. [Edmund] Muskie. We couldn't have a little operation and sort of change some identifying feature. We did try a salve called "Black No More" and it didn't work so we decided to make black beautiful. And that's why so many people are going to the Caribbean and getting suntan these days. We've got a major campaign on—since we can't become white, we're going to make white people black.

The others made it because there was a period when immigrants were given land. Because they came to this country during a time when all you needed was a strong back and a willing mind—before it became a highly technological and industrial age. They made it because they were not only given land but were given very good loans at low interest rates and then given farm agents by the Federal Government to teach them how to farm and now they are being given money not to farm. Others have made it because once they pursued a course of education and acquired some of the culture and some of the sophistication they could escape. They had freedom of choice. They could move where they want to. But a man, if he was black, regardless of his education, was caught in the ghetto. And so an Al Capone could move to Cicero, but a Ralph Bunch [United Nations diplomat and Nobel Peace Prize winner] could not and cannot now move to Cicero. Nor can he move to Bronxville, New York—and there are many Bronxvilles and Ciceros and Grosse Points that are much worse than some places in the South. They don't have a sign like some of the Southern cities used to have about "Nigger, don't let the sun set on you." . . .

What should we do? I think that we need to understand the mood. But more than the mood, we need to understand some of the language—what are people talking about when they shout "black power"? What is the significance behind decentralization which is something that all of you are going to have to face up to? We have had to face up to it in the Urban League. I suppose there was nobody who was more anxious for the slogan of "black power" to disappear the day after it was uttered than Whitney Young and all of us in the Urban League because we knew its overtones and the implications, the interpretations that would be given to it, of violence and of separatism. But it didn't go away—thanks to a sensation-seeking press and because it was born in an atmosphere of violence. So it seemed to us that we should take a hard look at it and try to sanitize it and try to give it a more constructive interpretation. There is really nothing new about the concept of a group seeking power. There is nothing new— every other group in American society has done it. To the Urban League, "black power" means first—"Look at me, I exist. I am somebody. I have pride. I have roots. I have an identity. I've made a contribution. I'm tired of being an invisible man, an asterisk in American life, a footnote." It says also that "I want the opportunity to participate in the decisions that affect my community—that if you want me to be responsible then give me responsibility and quit treating me like I am a colonial in American society." It says also that "We should organize our economic and political strength as all other groups have done to reward our friends and punish our enemies." The Irish did it, the Italians did it, the Catholics have done it, the Jews have done it, all other groups have done this. They just didn't make the mistake of shouting "Jewish power," "Italian power," or "Irish power"—the Irish just kept their mouths shut and took over the police departments of most cities in the country. And they made mistakes. They elected Curly, at first, not Jack Kennedy. Curly would make Adam Powell look like the epitome of political morality. All groups have made their mistakes and learned through trial and error and the black man should have the same opportunity to learn from trial and error. He will learn no other way. He has as much right to fail as anybody else. And incidentally, he has as much right to his crackpots as anybody else. There is no reason why white people should have a monopoly on crackpots. At least our crackpots don't go around bombing little children in churches and they don't go around denying to other human beings certain elementary rights. This is what decentralization is really all about.

The issue of separatism versus integration is an academic issue. For, the black poor of this country are, in fact, segregated. Almost without exception in the major cities of this country, black people are contained. The index of segregation has gone higher and higher and, today, we are a far more segregated society than we were twenty years ago. We do have in this country more of a condition of apartheid than one would want to admit. We aren't likely, overnight, to change this situation in spite of all of the good wishes and the laws. And in this segregated situation that we find ourselves, it is now clear that we will not be able to move into the mainstream and to compete with other Americans unless the institutions to which we are forced to accept services become not just equal but superior institutions. And those institutions cannot be run forever by outside absentee landlords and owners of business and policy makers in our schools. . . .

Black Leadership

If the responsible leadership in this country, black leadership, is denied this opportunity to show what we can do, then the country is in trouble. Because it immediately will fall into the clutches of the white and black revolutionists who have now formed a nice little alliance—the Black Panthers and the SDS [Students for a Democratic Society] people are working hand-in-hand today. And these are the people who say to the Whitney Youngs, "You know, you're a fool if you think that this problem can be worked out within the framework of this system. The system must be destroyed and its institutions must be destroyed." And they go farther and say, "We have no responsibility to provide alternatives, but this, we know, we must destroy."

Now, you will determine who are the prophets in history. Can the system be compassionate, intelligent enough, flexible enough to permit black people this kind of a piece of the action? I was down in Miami, Florida, not too long ago to the

AFL-CIO executive council meeting. I walked into the lobby of this very luxurious hotel and some of the labor leaders' wives were down there with their mink stoles and their Pekingese dogs. They were getting into their chauffeured limousines and they had just left their well-stocked suites upstairs. Their husbands were not up there debating on how to destroy the system, I can assure you. Forty years ago they were. But what had happened was, they had gotten a piece of the action, they had gotten a stake in the system. And you don't destroy that that you have a stake in. And that's the answer. When the black man in this country and the responsible leadership are given victories, then we can walk in the ghetto and say, "Cool it." And when asked "Why" we don't have to respond in terms of little token programs, or little "cool it" summer programs, or little pacifiers to keep the natives quiet; when we can talk about a massive program based upon a national commitment that's willing to appropriate the money like it did for the rebuilding of Western Europe and that sets a timetable on it that people can count on and not have their hopes raised only to be dashed by the passage of model cities legislation and rent supplements and poverty programs immediately to be sabotaged by the appropriation committee. And so no money goes out to amount to anything for model cities or rent supplements. The poverty program is supposed to be up around $8 billion now and it's barely creaking along at about a billion and a half while in every other area we are escalating. We spend much more money for the national guard and then, we kill a program of rat control.

The reason for this is that the leadership, the Congress today, hears from the lower middle class white person who is a victim of great fear. This guy who just made it on WPA and NYA, one generation removed from welfare, who is now saying, "We are against all these government programs." Rank and file union members who invented demonstrations and picketing and boycotting and violence in order to achieve their end are saying, "We're sick and tired of demonstrations. We're going to vote for [George] Wallace." They write to their congressmen. They proudly wear their Wallace buttons. But the nice decent people, you, the bankers, have up to very recent months distinguished yourselves by your thunderous silence and this has got to change. Not for my benefit, and the benefit of black people, but for the benefit of your country in which you have a greater stake than anybody else.

Equality in Employment

Now this means doing a lot of things. It means first of all making sure your own house is in order in terms of employment. As I look around this room, I would say that you've got an awful lot to do. I feel very much like Mr. Stanley looking for Dr. Livingston in Africa in reverse. I keep hoping I'll run across a credit official or bank loan official who is black. I finally met one, I think, this morning and I started to rush up to him and say, "Dr. Livingston, I presume." You can find them. Everybody else is finding them in industry generally. Some banks are in New York City. I know that there are some in Philadelphia. But obviously, if you are finding them you are not upgrading them or you are not taking those who you already have and upgrading them fast enough. Unless you do this, unless you get those road models, unless you get people in visible top spots then there will be no incentive and motivation. Don't come to the Urban League and say, "How do we motivate these people?" This is what an automobile manufacturer said to me not so long ago. "I hired, Whitney, 2,000 of those hard-core people you told me to but after the first pay day 500 quit. And they are late on Monday mornings, too." I told him we looked into this and we found that there was one institution where this didn't happen and that's in organized sports. Ever since Bill Russell became the head of the Boston Celtics (and that's like being president of AT&T in the commercial business), ever since Wilt Chamberlin began to make a couple hundred thousand dollars a year, ever since Willy Mays began to make a hundred and twenty-five thousand, we haven't had a single Negro basketball or baseball player to quit after the first pay day. We haven't had a single one late to work—there's no example of where they have been late to work on Monday mornings. So I said to him, "Who is your Willy Mays, who is the Bill Russell in your company." That's the answer. Black people are motivated like anyone else. They are motivated by the knowledge that through perseverance, extra study, and hard work they, too, can move upstairs.

And in our banks today like in a lot of other industries, you can still tell what floor you are on by the color—sort of checkerboard on the first floor, the basement is mainly black, but as you go up it gets whiter and whiter. So, I don't need to know what floor I'm on. I know I'm getting near the top just by the color of the employees for the most part. Except maybe for one instant black man who is out front to lead the way. Now this has to change. You can do it. You have the creative skills. I don't have to tell you how to do it. I did it in the Urban League in reverse. We had 1% white employees when I came in and now we've got 30%. And we did it through extra special recruiting techniques. We did it through lowering some of our standards that the white people couldn't meet. (I'm really not being completely facetious.) We wanted people who knew what it meant to be rejected. We wanted people who understood the language of the ghetto. We wanted people who understood the psychology of the poor. In our work this is a valid kind of qualification. Most white people couldn't meet it. And so we took in people like young Rusk, Secretary [of State Dean] Rusk's son, who was a Phi Beta Kappa from Cornell. We took in Adrian Zucker whose father was then head of the Air Force. We took in some law review graduates. Adrian was a Phi Beta Kappa from Radcliffe. We took Yale Law Review editors. We took bright people from public relations and from industrial relations. And we put them in a special provisional training course and gave them remedial teaching to help bring them up to our standards. I'm delighted to report that it works and that they are doing as well, if not better, than many of our black employees. But we were willing to change our screening process. We were willing to change some of our scores. We know you can't ask white people what to do when a rat comes in the room. How do you kill a bed bug? What's a syringe? What's chitlins? I mean, white people don't know anything about this. We have this intelligence test in Harlem that I sent to Scottie Reston (*New York Times*) the other day and he turned out to be an idiot, he said. He'd been taking the same kind of intelligence test based upon while middle class norms, about whether caviar smells like fish or fruit or whether you use red or white wine with chicken or steak and the slum kids don't know this. The tests aren't valid as a test of potential, as a test of intelligence.

Don't stop at just your jobs. Please do something about the attitudes, do something about housing, do something about education. You see, in the same breath that you tell me that you can't find any qualified people, you are also telling me how dumb you are because you are taxed twice. You pay the big taxes to maintain a public school system. And then you have to train people again for your companies. Why don't you get involved and see to it that these schools turn out people who can go to work for you right away? You need to disperse the housing and you play a crucial role in dispersal. You've got in New Haven and Newark now some banks who have set up a consortium in which they have set aside money for not just the development of black businesses but also for providing technical assistance and also for housing developments. And not all in the black community. I know it's better to get together collectively so one or two of you can't sneak out and appeal to the bigots. All of you feel a little scared. So what you do is get together so then they can't boycott any of you. All of you are in it together. That's what we had to do in Detroit and some other places. And this is what you've got to do to be credible to the black community. You are the one that suffers if this community becomes blacker and poorer. If people become tax eaters rather than tax producers, if people produce crime and welfare costs instead of producing goods and services, you pay the costs. And those are the sheer alternatives.

One final alternative is that you will either support responsible black leadership in this country or irresponsible leadership will take over. An organization like the Urban League that has been in business 58 years deserves better than what banks are doing for them now. Overnight, banks have given $100,000 to the Urban Coalition and then given the Urban League $5,000. Any kind of new idea that comes along they take off and say let's invest in that. You don't do that when it comes to building airplanes in time of war. You invest in Boeing and North America who've been producing airplanes. You don't go out and say let's start a new airplane manufacturing company. And yet when it comes to this problem the Urban League which tries to provide sane, intelligent, militantly responsible leadership does not get the resources to work with. The Urban League budgets ought to be quadrupled in these cities.

High Stakes

It isn't easy today to be a responsible leader. If you think you have to go home and apologize to somebody for associating with me, I want you to know that many times I have to apologize for associating with you. And I don't mind defending you to the black angry people in the ghetto (and that's not easy) if you don't mind defending me. Because we may have all come over here on different ships but at this moment we are in the same boat and we must never forget it. We'll sink or swim together. The stakes are high not just in terms of our cities and your banks. The stakes are high in terms of what kind of human being you want to be. What kind of husband, what kind of father.

I started talking about the children, let me close by talking about them. Mel Batton, who is chairman of the board of J.C. Penney, told me recently about his having breakfast one Sunday morning with his 21-year-old girl and his 23-year-old son. In just making conversation the girl said, "Where are you going this week, Dad?" And he said, "I'm going out with Whitney Young to three or four cities where I'm hosting some luncheons to talk about expanding employment opportunities for black people." And the boy almost fell off the stool and said, "You're going to do what?" And he explained it to him again. The boy said, "You mean you aren't going out this week and try to maximize the profits of J.C. Penney? You're not going out to find some product you can get a greater margin of profit on?" He said, "No." There was silence for a moment. And then his daughter with tears in her eyes jumped over and hugged and kissed him. And he said to me, "You know, Whitney, I've given my kids everything— cars, clothes, great allowances, tuitions, they've traveled all over the world." He said "but I never got more genuine respect and affection and love from my children than I got in that one moment." He said, "I want to thank you and the Urban League for giving me this opportunity to, for the first time, begin real communication with my child."

And that's what's at stake. These kids are serious today. They're not moved by money you give them. They know that you are getting ahead in your business and making money because of your own ambition, not because you want to give them more things. You say that but it is your own ambition, it's your own challenge. And they take it for granted just like my kids do. But the one thing they don't take for granted is when you tell them to stand up for what they believe in and not to conform to all the other kids but do what they know is right and then they turn around and they say, "But Mom and Daddy never do. They never stand up for what they believe in. They never lift their finger to get a black man a much better job or get a black man in the neighborhood or in the school. They are afraid."

Gentlemen, you teach by example and not by exhortation. You teach by precept and not by concept. And that's what's at stake. What kind of human being, what kind of man, what kind of American—this problem more than any other separates the real from the phony. An ancient Greek scholar was once asked to name when they would have justice in Athens. And he said, "We will have justice in Athens when those who are not injured are as indignant as those who are." And so shall it be in this society. We will have true justice in America when people like you who are not injured are as indignant as those who are.

CHAPTER
THREE

Strategies
and Tactics

A Call for Mass Action

A. Philip Randolph

A preeminent civil rights activist, A. Philip Randolph was also one of the most influential labor leaders of the twentieth century. In 1925 Randolph initiated a movement against the unfair labor policies of railroad companies. The resulting union, the Brotherhood of Sleeping Car Porters of which Randolph was president, ultimately secured a number of benefits for its members. In 1941, targeting discrimination in the defense industries, Randolph threatened President Franklin Roosevelt with a mass march on Washington, a rally that would bring fifty thousand blacks together in the nation's capital.

In the end, the march never took place; Roosevelt acquiesced to demands made by Randolph and other organizers and issued an executive order that prohibited discrimination in the armed services and defense plants. Nevertheless, the March on Washington Movement itself remained intact, and Randolph issued the following address at a special conference on September 27, 1942. An exceedingly eloquent speaker, Randolph outlines a strategy of mass action that in many ways anticipates much of the civil rights activism of the 1960s. Referring to the successes of the March on Washington Movement, Randolph urges blacks to use similar tactics—to band together in large numbers to make their voices heard—to combat racial discrimination. Randolph went on to become a key organizer of the famous 1963 March on Washington.

Excerpted from A. Philip Randolph's speech to a conference on the March on Washington Movement, Washington, DC, September 27, 1942.

Fellow Marchers and Delegates to the Policy Conference of the March on Washington Movement and Friends: We have met at an hour when the sinister shadows of war are lengthening and becoming more threatening. As one of the sections of the oppressed darker races, and representing a part of the exploited millions of the workers of the world, we are deeply concerned that the totalitarian legions of Hitler, Hirohito, and Mussolini do not batter the last bastions of democracy. We know that our fate is tied up with the fate of the democratic way of life. And so, out of the depth of our hearts, a cry goes up for the triumph of the United Nations. But we would not be honest with ourselves were we to stop with a call for a victory of arms alone. We know this is not enough. We fight that the democratic faiths, values, heritages and ideals may prevail.

Unless this war sounds the death knell to the old Anglo-American empire systems, the hapless story of which is one of exploitation for the profit and power of a monopoly capitalist economy, it will have been fought in vain. Our aim then must not only be to defeat Nazism, fascism, and militarism on the battlefield but to win the peace, for democracy, for freedom and the Brotherhood of Man without regard to his pigmentation, land of his birth or the God of his fathers. . . .

When this war ends, the people want something more than the dispersal of equality and power among individual citizens in a liberal, political democratic system. They demand with striking comparability the dispersal of equality and power among the citizen-workers in an economic democracy that will make certain the assurance of the good life—the more abundant life—in a warless world.

But, withal, this condition of freedom, equality and democracy is not the gift of the gods. It is the task of men, yes, men, brave men, honest men, determined men. . . .

The Goal of Equality

Thus our feet are set in the path toward [the long-range goal of] equality—economic, political and social and racial. Equality is the heart and essence of democracy, freedom and justice. Without equality of opportunity in industry, in labor

unions, schools and colleges, government, politics and before
the law, without equality in social relations and in all phases
of human endeavor, the Negro is certain to be consigned to
an inferior status. There must be no dual standards of justice,
no dual rights privileges, duties or responsibilities of citizenship. No dual forms of freedom. . . .

But our nearer goals include the abolition of discrimination, segregation, and Jim-Crow in the Government, the Army,
Navy, Air Corps, U.S. Marines, Coast Guard, Women's Aux-
iliary Army Corps and the Waves, and defense industries; the
elimination of discriminations in hotels, restaurants, on public
transportation conveyances, in educational, recreational, cultural, and amusement and entertainment places such as the-
atres, beaches, and so forth.

We want the full works of citizenship with no reservations. We will accept nothing less.

But goals must be achieved. They are not secured because
it is just and right that they be possessed by Negro or white
people. Slavery was not abolished because it was bad and unjust. It was abolished because men fought, bled and died on
the battlefield.

Therefore, if Negroes [are to] secure their goals, immediate and remote, they must win them and to win them they
must fight, sacrifice, suffer, go to jail and, if need be, die for
them. These rights will not be given. They must be taken.

Democracy was fought for and taken from political royalists—the kings. Industrial democracy, the rights of the
workers to organize and designate the representatives of their
own choosing to bargain collectively is being won and taken
from the economic royalists—big business.

Now the realization of goals and rights by a nation, race
or class requires belief in and loyalty to principles and policies. . . . Policies rest upon principles. Concretely a policy sets
forth one's position on vital public questions such as political
affiliations, religious alliances. The March on Washington
Movement must be opposed to partisan political commit-
ments, religious or denominational alliances. We cannot sup
with the Communists, for they rule or ruin any movement.
This is their policy. Our policy must be to shun them. This
does not mean that Negro Communists may not join the

March on Washington Movement.

As to the composition of our movement: Our policy is that it be all-Negro, and pro-Negro, but not anti-white, or anti-semitic, or anti-labor, or anti-Catholic. The reason for this policy is that all oppressed people must assume the responsibility and take the initiative to free themselves. Jews must wage their battle to abolish anti-semitism. Catholics must wage their battle to abolish anti-Catholicism. The workers must wage their battle to advance and protect their interests and rights.

But this does not mean that because Jews must take the responsibility and initiative to solve their own problems that they should not seek the cooperation and support of Gentiles, or that Catholics should not seek the support of Negroes, or that the workers should not attempt to enlist the backing of Jews, Catholics, and Negroes in their fight to win a strike; but the main reliance must be upon the workers themselves. By the same token because Negroes build an all-Negro movement such as the March, it does not follow that our movement should not call for the collaboration of Jews, Catholics, trade unions and white liberals to help restore the President's Fair Employment Practice Committee to its original status of independence, with responsibility to the President. That was done. William Green, President of the AF of L, and Philip Murray, President of CIO, were called upon to send telegrams to the President to restore the Committee to its independence. Both responded. Their cooperation had its effects. Workers have formed citizens committees to back them while on strike, but this does not mean that they take those citizens into their unions as members. No, not at all.

And while the March on Washington Movement may find it advisable to form a citizens committee of friendly white citizens to give moral support to a fight against the poll tax or white primaries, it does not imply that these white citizens or citizens of any racial group should be taken into the March on Washington Movement as members. The essential value of an all-Negro movement such as the March on Washington is that it helps to create faith by Negroes in Negroes. It develops a sense of self-reliance with Negroes depending on Negroes in vital matters. It helps to break down the slave psychology and inferiority complex in Negroes which comes and is nourished with Negroes relying on white people for direction and support. This inevitably happens in mixed organizations that are supposed to be in the interest of the Negro. . . .

Liberation of the Negro People

Therefore, while the March on Washington Movement is interested in the general problems of every community and will lend its aid to help solve them, it has as its major interest and task the liberation of the Negro people, and this is sound social economy. It is in conformity with the principle of the division of labor. No organization can do everything. Every organization can do something, and each organization is charged with the social responsibility to do that which it can do, it is built to do.

I have given quite some time to the discussion of this question of organizational structure and function and composition, because the March on Washington Movement is a mass movement of Negroes which is being built to achieve a definite objective, and is a departure from the usual pattern of Negro efforts and thinking. As a rule, Negroes do not choose to be to themselves in anything, they are only to themselves as a result of compulsive segregation. Negroes are together voluntarily for the same reason worker[s] join voluntarily into a trade union. But because workers only join trade unions, does not mean that the very same workers may not join organizations composed of some non-workers, such as art museums or churches or fraternal lodges that have varying purposes. This same thing is true of Negroes. Because Negroes only can join the March on Washington Movement, does not indicate that Negroes in the MOWM may not join an interracial golf club or church or Elks Lodge or debating society or trade union.

No one would claim that a society of Filipinos is undemocratic because it does not take in Japanese members, or that Catholics are anti-Jewish because the Jesuits won't accept Jews as members or that trade unions are illiberal because they deny membership to employers. Neither is the March on Washington Movement undemocratic because it confines its members to Negroes. Now this reasoning would not apply to a public school or a Pullman Car because these agencies are public in nature and provide a service which is necessary to all of the people of a community.

Now, the question of policy which I have been discussing involves, for example, the March on Washington Movement's position on the war. We say that the Negro must fight for his democratic rights now, for after the war it may be too late. This is our policy on the Negro and the war. But this policy raises the question of method, programs, strategy, and tactics; namely, how is this to be done. It is not sufficient to say that Negroes must fight for their rights now, during the war. Some methods must be devised, program set up, and strategy outlined.

This Policy Conference is designed to do this very thing. The first requirement to executing the policies of the March on Washington Movement is to have something to execute them with. This brings me to the consideration of organization. Organization supplies the power. The formulation of policies and the planning process furnish direction. Now there is organization and organization. Some people say, for instance, Negroes are already organized and they cite The Sisters of the Mysterious Ten, The Sons and Daughters of I Will Arise, the Holy Rollers, the social clubs, and so forth. But these organizations are concerned about the individual interest of helping the sick and funeralizing the dead or providing amusement and recreation. They deal with no social or racial problem which concerns the entire people. The Negro people as a whole is not interested in whether Miss A. plays Contract Bridge on Friday or not, or whether the deacon of the Methodist Church has a 200 or 500 dollar casket when he dies. These are personal questions. But the Negro race is concerned about Negroes being refused jobs in defense plants, or whether a Negro can purchase a lower in a Pullman Car, or whether the U.S. Treasury segregates Negro girls. Thus, while it is true Negroes are highly organized, the organizations are not built to deal with and manipulate the mechanics of power. Nobody cares how many Whist Clubs or churches or secret lodges Negroes establish because they are not compulsive or coercive. They don't seek to transform the socio-economic racial milieu. They accept and do not challenge conditions with an action program.

A Bold Action Program

Hence, it is apparent that the Negro needs more than organization. He needs mass organization with an action program, aggressive, bold and challenging in spirit. Such a movement is our March on Washington.

Our first job then is actually to organize millions of Negroes, and build them into block systems with captains so that they may be summoned to action overnight and thrown into physical motion. Without this type of organization, Negroes will never develop mass power which is the most effective weapon a minority people can wield. Witness the strategy and maneuver of the people of India with mass civil disobedience and non-cooperation and the marches to the sea to make salt. It may be said that the Indian people have not won their freedom. This is so, but they will win it. The central principle of the struggle of oppressed minorities like the Negro, labor, Jews, and others is not only to develop now, waging a world shaking, history making fight for independence. India's fight is the Negro's fight.

Now, let us be unafraid. We are fighting for big stakes. Our stakes are liberty, justice, and democracy. Every Negro should hang his head in shame who fails to do his part now for freedom. This is the hour of the Negro. It is the hour of the common man. May we rise to the challenge to struggle for our rights. Come what will or may, let us never falter.

Legal Strategies

Thurgood Marshall

As chief attorney for the National Association for the Advancement of Colored People (NAACP) from 1938 to 1961, Thurgood Marshall used the legal system to attack all forms of segregation—in housing laws, education, interstate travel, and voting rights. During these years, Marshall won twenty-nine cases before the Supreme Court, most notably the landmark *Brown v. the Topeka, Kansas Board of Education* in 1954, which ended state-enforced segregation in public schools. Marshall later became the first black justice of the Supreme Court.

In 1944 Marshall spoke at the NAACP Wartime Conference. His address, reprinted here, outlines the legal basis for civil rights. Describing specific legal strategies of the NAACP, Marshall exhorts blacks not only to use existing laws to their benefit, but also to press for the creation of new civil rights legislation.

T he struggle for full citizenship rights can be speeded by enforcement of existing statutory provisions protecting our civil rights. The attack on discrimination by use of legal machinery has only scratched the surface. An understanding of the existing statutes protecting our civil rights is necessary if we are to work toward enforcement of these statutes.

The titles "civil rights" and "civil liberties" have grown to include large numbers of subjects, some of which are properly included under these titles and others which should not be included. One legal treatise has defined the subject of civil rights as follows: "In its broadest sense, the term civil

Excerpted from Thurgood Marshall's speech to the NAACP Wartime Conference, July 13, 1944.

rights includes those rights which are the outgrowth of civilization, the existence and exercise of which necessarily follow from the rights that repose in the subjects of a country exercising self-government."

The Fourteenth and Fifteenth Amendments to the Constitution are prohibitions against action by the states and state officers violating civil rights. In addition to these provisions of the United States Constitution and a few others, there are several statutes of the United States which also attempt to protect the rights of individual citizens against private persons as well as public officers. Whether these provisions are included under the title of "civil rights" or "civil liberties" or any other subject is more or less unimportant as long as we bear in mind the provisions themselves.

All of the statutes, both federal and state, which protect the individual rights of Americans are important to Negroes as well as other citizens. Many of these provisions, however, are of peculiar significance to Negroes because of the fact that in many instances these statutes are the only protection to which Negroes can look for redress. It should also be pointed out that many officials of both state and federal governments are reluctant to protect the rights of Negroes. It is often difficult to enforce our rights when they are perfectly clear. It is practically impossible to secure enforcement of any of our rights if there is any doubt whatsoever as to whether or not a particular statute applies to the particular state of facts.

As to law enforcement itself, the rule as to most American citizens is that if there is any way possible to prosecute individuals who have willfully interfered with the rights of other individuals such prosecution is attempted. However, when the complaining party is a Negro, the rule is usually to look for any possible grounds for *not* prosecuting. It is therefore imperative that Negroes be thoroughly familiar with the rights guaranteed them by law in order that they may be in a position to insist that all of their fundamental rights as American citizens be protected.

The Thirteenth Amendment to the Constitution, abolishing slavery, the Fourteenth Amendment, prohibiting any action of state officials denying due process or the equal protection of its laws, and the Fifteenth Amendment, prohibiting discrimination by the states in voting are well-known to all of us. In addition to these provisions of the Constitution, there are the so-called Federal "Civil Rights Statutes" which include several Acts of Congress such as the Civil Rights Act and other statutes which have been amended from time to time and are now grouped together in several sections of the United States Code. The original Civil Rights Act was passed in Congress in 1866, but was vetoed by President Andrew Johnson the same year. It was, however, passed over the veto. It was reintroduced and passed in 1870 because there was some doubt as to its constitutionality, having been passed before the Fourteenth Amendment was ratified. The second bill has been construed several times and has been held constitutional by the United States Supreme Court, which in one case stated that "the plain objects of these statutes, as of the Constitution which authorized them, was to place the colored race, in respect to civil rights, upon a level with the whites. They made the rights and responsibilities, civil and criminal, of the two races exactly the same." (*Virginia v. Rives*, 100 U.S. 313 [1879])

The Thirteenth and Fourteenth and Fifteenth Amendments, along with the civil rights statutes protect the following rights:

1. Slavery is abolished and peonage is punishable as a federal crime. (13th amendment)
2. All persons born or naturalized in the U.S. are citizens and no state shall make or enforce any law abridging their privileges or immunities, or deny them equal protection of the law. (14th amendment)
3. The right of citizens to vote cannot be abridged by the United States or by any state on account of race or color. (15th amendment)
4. All persons within the jurisdiction of the United States shall have the same right to enforce contracts, or sue, be parties, give evidence, and to the full and equal benefit of all laws and proceedings as is enjoyed by white citizens.
5. All persons shall be subject to like punishment, pains, penalties, taxes, licenses, and extractions of every kind, and to no other.

6. All citizens shall have the same right in every state and territory, as is enjoyed by white citizens to inherit, purchase, lease, sell, hold and convey property.

7. Every person who, under color of statutes, custom or usage, subjects any citizen of the United States or person within the jurisdiction thereof to the deprivation of any rights, privileges, or immunities secured by the Constitution and laws is liable in an action at law, suit in equity, or other proper proceedings for redress.

8. Citizens possessing all other qualifications may not be disqualified from jury service in federal or state courts on account of race or color; any officer charged with the duty of selection or summoning of jurors who shall exclude citizens for reasons of race or color shall be guilty of a misdemeanor.

9. A conspiracy of two or more persons to deprive any person or class of persons of any rights guaranteed by constitution and laws is punishable as a crime and the conspirators are also liable in damages.

Most of these provisions only protect the citizen against wrong doing by public officials, although the peonage statutes and one or two others protect against wrongs by private persons.

Despite the purposes of these Acts which the United States Supreme Court insisted in 1879 "made the rights and responsibilities, civil and criminal, of the two races exactly the same," the experience of all of us points to the fact that this purpose has not as yet been accomplished. There are several reasons for this. In the first place, in certain sections of this country, especially in the deep south, judges, prosecutors and members of grand and petit juries, have simply refused to follow the letter or spirit of these provisions. Very often it happens that although the judge and prosecutor are anxious to enforce the laws, members of the jury are reluctant to protect the rights of Negroes. A third reason is that many Negroes themselves for one reason or another hesitate to avail themselves of the protection afforded by the United States Constitution and statutes.

These statutes protecting our civil rights in several instances provide for both criminal and civil redress. Some are criminal only and others are for civil action only. Criminal prosecution for violation of the federal statutes can be obtained only through the United States Department of Justice.

Enforcing Civil Rights Statutes

Up through and including the administration of Attorney General Homer S. Cummings, Negroes were unable to persuade the U.S. Department of Justice to enforce any of the civil rights statutes where Negroes were the complaining parties. The National Association for the Advancement of Colored People (NAACP) and its staff made repeated requests and in many instances filed detailed statements and briefs requesting prosecution for lynch mobs, persons guilty of peonage and other apparent violations of the federal statutes. It was not until the administration of Attorney General Frank Murphy that any substantial efforts were made to enforce the civil rights statutes as they apply to Negroes. Attorney General Murphy established a Civil Rights Section in the Department of Justice.

During the present administration of Attorney General Francis Biddle there have been several instances of prosecution of members of lynch mobs for the first time in the history of the United States Department of Justice. There have also been numerous successful prosecutions of persons guilty of peonage and slavery. However, other cases involving the question of the beating and killing of Negro soldiers by local police officers, the case involving the action of Sheriff Tip Hunter, of Brownsville, Tennessee, who killed at least one Negro citizen and forced several others to leave town, the several cases of refusal to permit qualified Negroes to vote, as well as other cases, have received the attention of the Department of Justice only to the extent of "investigating." Our civil rights as guaranteed by the federal statutes will never become a reality until the U.S. Department of Justice decides that it represents the entire United States and is not required to fear offending any section of the country which believes that it has the God-given right to be above the laws of the United States and the United States Supreme Court. . . .

There are, however, certain bright spots in the enforcement of the federal statutes. In addition to the lynching and peonage cases handled by the Washington office of the Department of Justice, there have been a few instances of courageous United States Attorneys in such places as Georgia who have vigorously prosecuted police officers who have used the power of their office as a cloak for beating up Negro citizens.

Using the Criminal Justice System

As a result of the recent decision in the Texas Primary Case, it is possible to use an example of criminal prosecution under the civil rights statutes by taking a typical case of the refusal to permit the Negroes to vote in the Democratic Primary elections. Let us see how a prosecution is started: In Waycross, Georgia, for example, we will suppose a Negro elector on July 4, 1944, went to the polls with his tax receipt and demanded to vote in the Democratic Primary. He should, of course, have witnesses with him. Let us also assume that the election officials refused to let him vote solely because of his race or color.

As a matter of law, the election officials violated a federal criminal law and are subject to fine and imprisonment. But how should the voter or the organized Negro citizens, or the local NAACP Branch go about trying to get the machinery of criminal justice in motion? Of course, the details of what happens must be put in writing and sworn to by the person who tried to vote and also by his witnesses. Then the matter must be placed before the United States Attorney. This is the *federal* district attorney.

I wonder how many of the delegates here know who is the United States Attorney for their district, or even where his office is. Every Branch should know the United States Attorney for that area, even if a delegation goes in just to get acquainted and let him know that we expect him to enforce the civil rights laws with the same vigor as used in enforcing other criminal statutes.

But back to the voting case. The affidavits must be presented to the United States Attorney with a demand that he investigate and place the evidence before the Federal Grand Jury. At the same time copies of the affidavits and statements in the case should be sent to the National Office. We will see that they get to the Attorney General in Washington. I wish that I could guarantee you that the Attorney General would put pressure on local United States Attorneys who seem reluctant to prosecute. At least we can assure you that we will give the Attorney General no rest unless he gets behind these reluctant United States attorneys throughout the south.

There is no reason why a hundred clear cases of this sort should not be placed before the United States Attorneys and the Attorney General every year until the election officials discover that it is both wiser and safer to follow the United States laws than to violate them. It is up to us to see that these officials of the Department of Justice are called upon to act again and again wherever there are violations of the civil rights statutes. Unfortunately, there are plenty of such cases. It is equally unfortunate that there are not enough individuals and groups presenting these cases and demanding action.

The responsibility for enforcement of the civil provisions of the civil rights statutes rests solely with the individual. In the past we have neglected to make full use of these statutes. Although they have been on the books since 1870, there were very few cases under these statutes until recent years. Whereas in the field of general law there are many, many precedents for all other types of action, there are very few precedents for the protection of civil liberties.

The most important of the civil rights provisions is the one which provides that "every person who, under color of any statute, ordinance, regulation, custom or usage of any state or territory subjects or causes to be subjected any citizen of the United States or person within the jurisdiction thereof to the deprivation of any rights, privileges or immunities secured by the Constitution and laws shall be liable to the party injured in an action at law, suit in equity or other proper proceeding for redress." Under this statute any officer of a state, county or municipality who while acting in an official capacity, denies to any citizen or person within the state any of the rights guaranteed by the Constitution or laws is subject to a civil action. This statute has been used to equalize teachers' salaries and to obtain bus transportation for Negro school children. It can be used to attack *every* form of discrimination against Negroes by public school systems. . . .

This statute, along with other of the civil rights statutes, can be used to enforce the right to register and vote throughout the country. The threats of many of the bigots in the south to disregard the ruling of the Supreme Court of the United States in the recent Texas Primary decision has not intimidated a single person. The United States Supreme Court remains the highest court in this land. Election officials in states affected by this decision will either let Negroes vote in the Democratic Primaries, or they will be subjected to both criminal and civil prosecution under the civil rights statutes. In every state in the deep south Negroes have this year attempted to vote in the primary elections. Affidavits concerning the refusal to permit them to vote in Alabama, Florida and Georgia have already been sent to the United States Department of Justice. We will insist that these election officials be prosecuted and will also file civil suits against the guilty officials.

It can be seen from these examples that we have just begun to scratch the surface in the fight for full enforcement of these statutes. The NAACP can move no faster than the individuals who have been discriminated against. We only take up cases where we are requested to do so by persons who have been discriminated against.

Segregation

Another crucial problem is the ever-present problem of segregation. Whereas the principle has been established by cases handled by the NAACP that neither states nor municipalities can pass ordinances segregating residences by race, the growing problem today is the problem of segregation by means of restrictive covenants, whereby private owners band together to prevent Negro occupancy of particular neighborhoods. Although this problem is particularly acute in Chicago, it is at the same time growing in intensity throughout the country. It has the full support of the real estate boards in the several cities, as well as most of the banks and other leading agencies. The legal attack on this problem has met with spotty success. In several instances restrictive covenants have been declared invalid because the neighborhood has changed, or for other reasons. Other cases have been lost. However, the NAACP is in the process of preparing a detailed memorandum and will establish procedure which will lead to an all-out legal attack on restrictive covenants. Whether or not this attack will be successful cannot be determined at this time.

The National Housing Agency and the Federal Public Housing Authority have established a policy of segregation in federal public housing projects. A test case has been filed in Detroit, Mich., and is still pending in the local federal courts. The Detroit situation is the same as in other sections of the country. Despite the fact that the Housing Authority and other agencies insist that they will maintain separate but equal facilities, it never develops that the separate facilities are equal in all respects. In Detroit separate projects were built and it developed that by the first of this year every single white family in the area eligible for public housing had been accommodated and there were still some 800 "white" units vacant with "no takers." At the same time there were some 45,000 Negroes inadequately housed and with no units open to them. This is the inevitable result of "separate but equal" treatment. . . .

States with Civil Rights Statutes

We should also be mindful of the several so-called civil rights statutes in the several states. There are civil rights acts in at least 18 states, all of which are in the north and middle west. These statutes are in California, Colorado, Connecticut, Illinois, Indiana, Iowa, Kansas, Massachusetts, Michigan, Minnesota, Nebraska, New Jersey, New York, Ohio, Pennsylvania, Rhode Island and Washington. California provides only for civil action. Illinois, Kansas, Minnesota, New York and Ohio have both civil and criminal provisions. In New Jersey the only action is a criminal action, or an action for penalty in the name of the state, the amount of the penalty going to the state.

In those states not having civil rights statutes it is necessary that every effort be made to secure passage of one. In states having weak civil rights statutes efforts should be made to have them strengthened. In states with reasonably strong civil rights statutes, like Illinois and New York, it is necessary that every effort be made to enforce them. . . .

Outside of New York City there are very few successful cases against the civil rights statutes because of the fact that members of the jury are usually reluctant to enforce the statutes. I understand the same is true for Illinois. The only method of counteracting this vicious practice is by means of educating the general public, from which juries are chosen, to the plight of the Negro.

It should also be pointed out that many of our friends of other races are not as loud and vociferous as the enemies of our race. In northern and mid-western cities it repeatedly happens that a prejudiced southerner on entering a hotel or restaurant, seeing Negroes present makes an immediate and loud protest to the manager. It is very seldom that any of our friends go to the managers of places where Negroes are excluded and complain to them of this fact. Quite a job can be done if our friends of other races will only realize the importance of this problem and get up from their comfortable chairs and actually go to work on the problem.

Thus it seems clear that although it is necessary and vital to all of us that we continue our program for additional legislation to guarantee and enforce certain of our rights, at the same time we must continue with ever-increasing vigor to enforce those few statutes, both federal and state, which are now on the statute books. We must not be delayed by people who say "the time is not ripe," nor should we proceed with caution for fear of destroying the "status quo." Persons who deny to us our civil rights should be brought to justice now. Many people believe the time is always "ripe" to discriminate against Negroes. All right then—the time is always "ripe" to bring them to justice. The responsibility for the enforcement of these statutes rests with every American citizen regardless of race or color. However, the real job has to be done by the Negro population with whatever friends of the other races are willing to join in.

Federal Civil Rights Legislation

John F. Kennedy

The civil rights movement gained a powerful ally when John F. Kennedy was elected to the presidency in 1960. Although a strong supporter of black causes, Kennedy did not focus on racial problems in the first two years of his administration. In 1963, however, a series of turbulent events in Birmingham, Alabama, where major desegregation campaigns were unfolding, grabbed the attention of the president—and the entire nation. Then, when Alabama governor George Wallace, an ardent segregationist, defied orders to integrate the University of Alabama, Kennedy took action, federalizing Alabama National Guard troops to ensure the peaceful admission of two black students. The next night, June 11, 1963, Kennedy delivered a nationally televised address to comment on his actions in Birmingham, to endorse civil rights activism in general, and to promote federal civil rights legislation as a means of securing black rights. Kennedy's speech, reprinted here, remains one of the most important presidential addresses on civil rights in American history.

This nation was founded by men of many nations and backgrounds. It was founded on the principle that all men are created equal; and that the rights of every man are diminished when the rights of one man are threatened.

It ought to be possible, therefore, for American students of any color to attend any public institution they select with-

Excerpted from John F. Kennedy's national address, June 11, 1963.

out having to be backed up by troops. It ought to be possible for American consumers of any color to receive equal service in places of public accommodation, such as hotels and restaurants, and theaters and retail stores, without being forced to resort to demonstrations in the street.

And it ought to be possible for American citizens of any color to register and to vote in a free election without interference or fear of reprisal.

It ought to be possible, in short, for every American to enjoy the privileges of being American without regard to his race or his color.

This is not a sectional issue. Difficulties over segregation and discrimination exist in every city, in every state of the Union, producing in many cities a rising tide of discontent that threatens the public safety.

Nor is this a partisan issue. In a time of domestic crisis, men of goodwill and generosity should be able to unite regardless of party or politics.

This is not even a legal or legislative issue alone. It is better to settle these matters in the courts than on the streets,

John F. Kennedy was a strong supporter of civil rights. In this picture, black voters line up to shake his hand during his campaign for the presidency.

and new laws are needed at every level. But law alone cannot make men see right.

A Moral Issue

We are confronted primarily with a moral issue. It is as old as the Scriptures and is as clear as the American Constitution. The heart of the question is whether all Americans are to be afforded equal rights and equal opportunities; whether we are going to treat our fellow Americans as we want to be treated.

If an American, because his skin is dark, cannot eat lunch in a restaurant open to the public; if he cannot send his children to the best public schools available; if he cannot vote for the public officials who represent him; if, in short, he cannot enjoy the full and free life which all of us want, then who among us would be content to have the color of his skin changed and stand in his place?

Who among us would then be content with the counsels of patience and delay? One hundred years of delay have passed since President Lincoln freed the slaves, yet their heirs, their grandsons, are not fully free. They are not yet freed from the bonds of injustice; they are not yet freed from social and economic oppression.

And this nation, for all its hopes and all its boasts, will not be fully free until all its citizens are free.

Now the time has come for this nation to fulfill its promise. The events in Birmingham and elsewhere have so increased the cries for equality that no city or state or legislative body can prudently choose to ignore them.

The fires of frustration and discord are burning in every city, North and South. Where legal remedies are not at hand, redress is sought in the streets in demonstrations, parades and protests, which create tensions and threaten violence— and threaten lives.

We face, therefore, a moral crisis as a country and a people. It cannot be met by repressive police action. It cannot be left to increased demonstrations in the streets. It cannot be quieted by token moves or talk. It is a time to act in the Congress, in your state and local legislative body, and, above all, in all of our daily lives.

A Call for Legislation

I am, therefore, asking the Congress to enact legislation giving all Americans the right to be served in facilities which are open to the public—hotels, restaurants and theaters, retail stores and similar establishments. This seems to me to be an elementary right.

I'm also asking Congress to authorize the Federal Government to participate more fully in lawsuits designed to end segregation in public education. We have succeeded in persuading many districts to desegregate voluntarily. Dozens have admitted Negroes without violence.

Other features will also be requested, including greater protection for the right to vote.

But legislation, I repeat, cannot solve this problem alone. It must be solved in the homes of every American in every community across our country.

In this respect, I want to pay tribute to those citizens, North and South, who've been working in their communities to make life better for all.

They are acting not out of a sense of legal duty but out of a sense of human decency. Like our soldiers and sailors in all parts of the world, they are meeting freedom's challenge on the firing line, and I salute them for their honor—their courage.

Beyond Nonviolence

John Lewis

Following President John F. Kennedy's televised address
calling for civil rights legislation in June 1963, many
blacks became more assertive in their demands for social
and economic change. At the same time, with resistance
to the civil rights movement fierce, a growing faction of
blacks was becoming dissatisfied with the government's
attempt to keep the fight for rights in the courts. John
Lewis, then chairman of the Student Nonviolent Coordinating Committee (SNCC), was a particularly vocal opponent of the Kennedy administration and its civil rights
bill. In a speech delivered at the March on Washington,
Lewis expresses his suspicion of the federal government
and its inadequate measures to fight racism. With his impassioned mantra of "revolution is at hand," Lewis exhorts blacks to use bolder strategies to dismantle "the
chains of political and economic slavery."

We march today for jobs and freedom, but we have
nothing to be proud of, for hundreds and thousands of our brothers are not here—for they have
no money for their transportation, for they are receiving star-
vation wages . . . or no wages at all.

In good conscience, we cannot support the administra-
tion's civil-rights bill, for it is too little, and too late. There's not
one thing in the bill that will protect our people from police
brutality. [Because of objections by some of the march's spon-
sors, this was changed to read: "True, we support the administration's civil-rights bill, but this bill will not protect young
children and old women from police dogs and fire hoses. . . ."]

Excerpted from John Lewis's speech at the March on Washington, Washington, DC,
August 28, 1963.

The voting section of this bill will not help the thousands of citizens who want to vote; will not help the citizens of Mississippi, of Alabama and Georgia who are qualified to vote, who are without a sixth-grade education. "One Man, One Vote," is the African cry. It is ours, too.

People have been forced to move for they have exercised their right to register to vote. What is in the bill that will protect the homeless and starving people of this nation? What is there in this bill to insure the equality of a maid who earns five dollars a week in the home of a family whose income is a hundred thousand dollars a year?

This bill will not protect young children and old women from police dogs and fire hoses for engaging in peaceful demonstrations. This bill will not protect the citizens in Danville, Virginia, who must live in constant fear in a police state. [In Danville, Virginia, policemen, armed with submachine guns and in armored cars, regularly broke up mass demonstrations by Negroes. After each demonstration, scores of Negroes were taken to hospitals with fractured skulls and lacerations.] This bill will not protect the hundreds of people who have been arrested on trumped-up charges, like those in Americus, Georgia, where four young men are in jail, facing a death penalty, for engaging in peaceful protest.

For the first time in a hundred years this nation is being awakened to the fact that segregation is evil and it must be destroyed in all forms. Our presence today proves that we have been aroused to the point of action.

Revolution

We are now involved in a serious revolution. This nation is still a place of cheap political leaders allying themselves with open forms of political, economic and social exploitation.

In some parts of the South we have worked in the fields from sun-up to sun-down for twelve dollars a week. In Albany, Georgia, we have seen our people indicted by the federal government for peaceful protest, while the Deputy Sheriff beat Attorney C.B. King and left him half-dead; while local police officials kicked and assaulted the pregnant wife of Slater King, and she lost her baby.

It seems to me that the Albany indictment is part of a conspiracy on the part of the federal government and local politicians for political expediency.

I want to know, Which side is the federal government on?

The revolution is at hand, and we must free ourselves of the chains of political and economic slavery. The nonviolent

At the 1963 March on Washington, pictured here, John Lewis urged blacks to use bolder strategies to fight racism.

revolution is saying, "We will not wait for the courts to act, for we have been waiting hundreds of years. We will not wait for the President, nor the Justice Department, nor Congress, but we will take matters into our own hands, and create a great source of power, outside of any national structure that could and would assure us victory." For those who have said, "Be patient and wait!" we must say, "Patience is a dirty and nasty word." We cannot be patient, we do not want to be free gradually, we want our freedom, and we want it now. We cannot depend on any political party, for both the Democrats and the Republicans have betrayed the basic principles of the Declaration of Independence.

We all recognize the fact that if any radical social, political and economic changes are to take place in our society, the people, the masses must bring them about. In the struggle we must seek more than mere civil rights; we must work for the community of love, peace and true brotherhood. Our minds, souls and hearts cannot rest until freedom and justice exist for *all the people*.

Black Masses on the March

The revolution is a serious one. Mr. Kennedy is trying to take the revolution out of the streets and put it in the courts. Listen, Mr. Kennedy, listen, Mr. Congressman, listen, fellow citizens—the black masses are on the march for jobs and freedom, and we must say to the politicians that there won't be a "cooling-off period."

We won't stop now. All of the forces of Eastland, Barnett and Wallace won't stop this revolution. The next time we march, we won't march on Washington, but we will march through the South, through the Heart of Dixie, the way Sherman did. We will make the action of the past few months look petty. And I say to you, *Wake up America!!*

All of us must get in the revolution—get in and stay in the streets of every city, village and hamlet of this nation, until true freedom comes, until the revolution is complete. The black masses in the Delta of Mississippi, in Southwest Georgia, Alabama, Harlem, Chicago, Philadelphia and all over this nation are on the march.

Positive Action Programs

Roy Wilkins

Roy Wilkins joined the National Association for the Advancement of Colored People (NAACP) as assistant secretary in 1931 and served as the organization's executive director from 1955 to 1977. In his forty-six years with the NAACP, Wilkins remained a steadfast proponent of using legal channels and direct action protest to promote social change, an approach criticized by more militant blacks who found his moderate campaign insufficient in the fight against racism.

On July 5, 1966, Wilkins delivered the keynote address to the annual convention of the NAACP. In forceful language, Wilkins explains why he is morally opposed to the often violent, separatist notions of "black power" and reiterates his commitment to the full inclusion of blacks in American society. To this end, Wilkins advocates a program for social change that operates within the bounds of law, citing expanded NAACP social action programs and community involvement. An excerpt from Wilkins's speech is reprinted here.

N o matter how endlessly they try to explain it, the term "black power" means anti-white power. In a racially pluralistic society, the concept, the formation and the exercise of an ethnically-tagged power, means opposition to other ethnic powers, just as the term "white supremacy" means subjection of all non-white people. In the black-white relationship, it has to mean that every other ethnic power is the rival and the antagonist of "black power." It has to mean "going-it-alone." It has to mean separatism.

Now, separatism, whether on the rarefied debate level of "black power" or on the wishful level of a secessionist Freedom City in Watts, offers a disadvantaged minority little except the chance to shrivel and die.

The only possible dividend of "black power" is embodied in its offer to millions of frustrated and deprived and persecuted black people of a solace, a tremendous psychological lift, quite apart from its political and economic implications.

Race Against Race

Ideologically it dictates "up with black and down with white" in precisely the same fashion that South Africa reverses that slogan.

It is a reverse Mississippi, a reverse Hitler, a reverse Ku Klux Klan.

If these were evil in our judgment, what virtue can be claimed for black over white? If, as some proponents claim, this concept instills pride of race, cannot this pride be taught without preaching hatred or supremacy based upon race?

Though it be clarified and clarified again, "black power" in the quick, uncritical and highly emotional adoption it has received from some segments of a beleaguered people can mean in the end only black death. Even if, through some miracle, it should be enthroned briefly in an isolated area, the human spirit, which knows no color or geography or time, would die a little, leaving for wiser and stronger and more compassionate men the painful beating back to the upward trail.

We of the NAACP will have none of this. We have fought it too long. It is the ranging of race against race on the irrelevant basis of skin color. It is the father of hatred and the mother of violence.

It is the wicked fanaticism which has swelled our tears, broken our bodies, squeezed our hearts and taken the blood of our black and white loved ones. It shall not now poison our forward march.

We seek, therefore, as we have sought these many years,

the inclusion of Negro Americans in the nation's life, not their exclusion. This is our land, as much so as it is any American's—every square foot of every city and town and village. The task of winning our share is not the easy one of disengagement and flight, but the hard one of work, of short as well as long jumps, of disappointments, and of sweet successes.

In our Fight for Freedom we choose:

1. The power and the majesty of the ballot, the participation of free men in their government, both as voters and as honorable and competent elected and appointed public servants. Year in and year out, the NAACP voter registration work has proceeded. No one except the Federal Government has registered more Negro voters in Mississippi than the NAACP. In six weeks last summer more than twenty thousand new names were added by our workers alone, with additional thousands during an intensive renewal last winter. That work is continuing under the leadership of our Mississippi state president, Dr. Aaron Henry, and of our state director, Charles Evers. Later this month a summer task force will be at work in Louisiana. Already our South Carolina NAACP is busy on registration, as is our Alabama organization.

We are aware that a Louisiana young man, born along the Mississippi border, has been named and confirmed as one of the seven governors of the Federal Reserve Bank. We know that his extraordinary ability finally tipped the scales, but we know also, that, without ballot power, he would not even have been on the scales ready to be tipped.

2. We choose employment for our people—jobs not hidden by racial labels or euphemisms, not limited by racial restrictions in access and promotion, whether by employers or organized labor. We commend a growing number of corporations for expanding their employment of Negro applicants in technical and professional posts, but we insist that only the surface has been scratched.

Barriers in Employment

We commend the "good guys" among the trade unions for the improvement in opportunities and advancement for the Negro worker, but we condemn the policies of some unions which have either barred or heavily handicapped the Negro worker. Negro employment is in a crisis stage. The rate of unemployment ranges from twice that of whites to four and five times the white rate in some areas. The answer to the complaint of employers that workers are not trained is to institute in-plant training, just as they have in other shortages. The apprentice training stranglehold must be broken, the racially separate seniority lines, the still-persisting segregated local and the remaining crude segregation in plant facilities must be abolished. The demonstrations before the U.S. Steel Corporation offices and plants under the cooperative leadership of Dr. John Nixon, our Alabama president, and Henry Smith, our Pennsylvania president, had wide and beneficial impact.

The Negro migrant worker, the forgotten man in the employment picture, must have attention.

In the Watts district of Los Angeles last year the unemployment rate was more than 30 per cent, a rate higher than that during the great, nationwide Depression of the Nineteen Thirties. The Negro teenage rate is nearly 25 per cent as against 13 per cent for white teenagers.

Negro employment is a disaster area demanding the strict enforcement of Title VII of the 1964 Civil Rights Act. The NAACP has filed more than one thousand complaints with the Equal Employment Opportunity Commission and will file more until the law accomplishes what it was enacted to do. As evidence of his continuing concern, Congressman Augustus Hawkins of Los Angeles succeeded in having his bill relating to federal employment passed by the House as an amendment to Title VII of the 1964 Civil Rights Act.

3. We choose to combat the color line in housing. In one breath our opinion-makers decry the existence of the poverty and filth and crime and degradation of the slums, but in the next they decry low-cost housing and fair housing laws. Here in California the hysteria over whether Negro Americans should live in gullies or be pushed into the sea reached the Proposition 14 stage which the state's highest court has declared unconstitutional. But who cares about the Constitution when a Negro might be enabled to move into the neighborhood? One could think black Americans were men from Mars. Instead, we have been here, side by side with the white

folks (some of whom just got here), for 345 years.

They tell us to work hard and save our money, to go to school and prepare ourselves, to be "responsible," to rear and educate our children in a wholesome and directed family atmosphere, to achieve, to "get up in the world."

After we do all this, they look us in the eye and bar us from renting or buying a home that matches our achievements and one in keeping with our aspirations for further advancement.

Some public officials, including mayors of cities, and many candidates for election to public office are not above public double talk and private single talk on this issue. Any candidate who orates

Roy Wilkins

about basic Americanism or "the American way," but who hems and haws over fair housing legislation is no friend of the Negro citizen.

The Administration's civil rights bill of 1966 with its vital section barring discrimination in the rental or sale of housing must be enacted with the amendment, already inserted by the committee, providing for administrative redress as well as court action.

Your congressmen and senators are at home until July 11 celebrating Independence Day—Freedom Day for the United States. See them or have your branch officers back home see them in person. Urge them to rub some freedom off on twenty million loyal Americans by voting for a strong civil rights bill. Of course the section on punishing in the federal courts those who attack civil rights workers must pass. And we must have indemnification for victims.

4. Most of all, we choose to secure unsegregated, high quality public education for ourselves and our children. A new report, made public only last week, is a jolt for anyone who thought the 1954 Supreme Court decision or subsequent legislation solved the problem.

The report says officially and professionally what we have contended all along: that predominantly Negro schools are inferior to those attended largely by whites. Also that the achievement gap widens between the first grade and the twelfth. In other words, the longer our children attend racially segregated schools, the farther they fall behind white children.

And, lest the non-Southerners feel smug, the report found that segregation for both whites and Negroes is more complete in the South, but "is extensive in other regions where the Negro population is concentrated: the urban North, Midwest and West."

The Federal Government, whose Office of Education has made some strong statements, must follow up with a strong enforcement of Title VI of the 1964 law. The empty promises of school officials and the defiance of the whole State of Alabama must not be accepted meekly by federal officials. The furor over the guidelines issued by HEW is another version of the Dixie bluff on race which has worked so well for so many decades. The guidelines are mild. They are legal and not illegal as Governor Wallace proclaimed to his state's educators. They ask the Southerners to do what is for them a strange thing: obey the school desegregation law. On this point the Federal Government must not yield. The Attorney General and the Department of Justice must back up resolutely the legality of federal action. There can be no temporizing.

Outside the South the call is for unrelenting activity to wipe out de facto school segregation. Boston, Massachusetts, has proved to be the Mississippi of the North. In fact, in fairness to Mississippi and in consideration of the starting points and traditions of the two places, Boston is *below* Mississippi on this issue. The details, the traps, the methods and the progress will be covered in workshop discussions, but here it must be said that before we can get jobs to earn increased income to buy and rent better homes, before we can contribute to the enrichment of our nation, we must have free access to quality education.

The man who shoots and burns and drowns us is surely our enemy, but so is he who cripples our children for life with inferior public education.

Urban Problems

5. We also choose to wrestle with the complex problems of urban life, all of which include an attitude toward and a treatment of millions of Negro citizens. The solution of urban problems will become the solution of living in the last third of our century since more than 70 per cent of Americans now live in urban communities.

If it has been asked once, it has been asked a hundred times: Are we going to have a long, hot summer? The answer has many facets, some extremely complex and difficult. But one quick answer is that the police everywhere can make or break urban racial tensions by their conduct toward minority group citizens.

Last summer [1965] you had here an upheaval that shook the world [four days of rioting in Watts]. To many of us who looked from afar, it appeared to be a wild, senseless rampage of hate and destruction. But that was far from the whole truth.

There was powder in Watts, piled up and packed down through the years: wide-scale unemployment, both adult and teenage, slum housing, crowded schools, non-existent health facilities, inadequate transportation and—the Parker police attitude. Everyone was suspect and everyone was subject to harassment in one form or another. The community smoldered under the peculiar brand that police place upon a whole section with their constant sirens, their contemptuous searches, their rough talk, their ready guns and their general "Godalmightiness."

The lesson they and city officials have learned from last year is to seek not correction and improvement, but still more repression. Mayor Yorty and whoever writes his scripts testified in Sacramento in support of a so–called riot–control bill.

The only thing one has to remember about this bill is that it would allow a policeman to judge whether an utterance or an act is an incitement to riot! On his own judgment he could arrest or club or otherwise deter—or shoot—a person whom he (not the law or the courts) deemed to be an inciter of riot. Down the drain goes freedom of speech and down, too, possibly, goes a life.

The McCone Report on the 1965 riot called for "costly and extreme" remedies for Watts, undertaken with a "revolutionary attitude." The answer of the City of Los Angeles was to vote down a hospital bond issue. The answer of Mayor Yorty and of his man, Chief Parker, is a trampling-tough riot-control bill which, if enacted, would loose the police, almost without restraint, upon a populace sick to death—literally—of race control. To blot out any remaining fitful light, one of the gubernatorial candidates, full of disavowals, is the darling of those ultraconservatives who believe in iron control of what they call "violence in the streets"—their code name for Negroes.

If this is the best that a great city can bring to a hard urban problem, one largely of its own making, then God pity both the whites and the Negroes!

We have no panacea for all these problems. We do not proclaim that what we declare here this week is going to change the course of the whole civil rights movement. We do not know all the answers to the [Governor] George Wallace problem in Alabama, the [Senator] James Eastland problem in Mississippi, or to the Boston, Massachusetts, school committee and its [Representative] Louise Day Hicks problem. We certainly don't know the answers to foreign policy and to tax and interest rate puzzlers.

NAACP Programs

But in this unsettled time when shifts are the order of the day and when change is in the air, we can sail our NAACP ship "steady as she goes," with more drive to the turbines, more skill at the wheel, but no fancy capers for the sake of capers.

We can follow down into each community the really advanced blueprint of the White House Conference "To Fulfill These Rights," which covered four principal areas: economic security and welfare, education, housing, and the administration of justice.

We can expand and point up the community services of our NAACP branches, each of which is, in reality, a citizenship clinic. Just as medical clinics need specialists to cure physical ills, so our branch clinics should recruit volunteer specialists to diagnose and minister to social ills.

We must involve people in the communities in the solution of our problem—not limiting ourselves to our church or lodge or club group.

We must keep the pressure on our local and state education systems through the employment of every legitimate technique: protests, surveys, discussions, demonstrations, picketing and negotiation. Nothing should be overlooked in fighting for better education. Be persistent and ornery; this will be good for the lethargic educational establishment and will aid the whole cause of public education.

Our branches are at work in their territories. In Baltimore, the NAACP won a case against the police commissioner which the Fourth Circuit Court of Appeals declared revealed the most flagrant police practices ever to come before the court. The Blair County, Pennsylvania, NAACP is busy rooting out the remaining discrimination in public accommodations in Clearfield, Pennsylvania.

The Wilmington, Ohio, NAACP has a program for tutoring adults and drop-outs and has recruited college professors and students and textbooks to make the project effective. The Bay City, Michigan, NAACP also has a tutorial program under way as well as continuous work on industrial employment practices and housing. The Stillwater, Oklahoma, NAACP is active on a child care center project and on high school desegregation.

And the Montgomery County, West Virginia, NAACP, bless its heart, is 112 per cent above last year in membership and 500 per cent above last year in funds raised.

Thirty-one branches found time and funds to be present at the [James] Meredith march rally in Jackson, Mississippi, even though the Association, at the last minute, was insulted by the barring of Charles Evers as an NAACP spokesman.

This is only part of the chronicle of "steady as she goes." In a world where the Mayor of Los Angeles is yelling "riot control," where Rhodesia says "never!" to black representation while in America SNCC raises the chant of black power, where the Federal Government at long last is committed, but both the far right and the far left offer vocal and vicious objection, someone has to drive the long haul toward the group goal of Negro Americans and the larger ideal of our young nation.

Our objective is basically as it was laid down in 1909 by the interracial founders of our NAACP. Back there William Lloyd Garrison [speaker means Oswald Garrison Villard] expressed the strong feeling that the first NAACP conference "will utter no uncertain sound on any point affecting the vital subject. No part of it is too delicate for plain speech. The republican experiment is at stake, every tolerated wrong to the Negro reacting with double force upon white citizens guilty of faithlessness to their brothers."

As it was then, so it is today. The republican experiment *is* at stake in 1966. More than that, the dream of a brotherhood in equality and justice is imperiled.

Our fraternity tonight, as it was then, is the fraternity of man, not the white, or brown, or yellow, or black man, but man.

The Voting Rights Act

Lyndon B. Johnson

Lyndon B. Johnson became president of the United States after President John F. Kennedy was assassinated on November 22, 1963. Although many feared that the famous civil rights legislation would languish in Congress without Kennedy's support, Johnson continued to rally for its passage; on July 2, President Johnson signed the Civil Rights Act of 1964 into law. Despite voting rights provisions in the new legislation, a great majority of southern blacks avoided the polls. Literacy tests, poll taxes, and the general threat of violence and economic hardship, for example, kept many blacks from exercising their right to vote.

Calling for new legislation to combat those abuses, Johnson delivered an address before a joint session of Congress on March 15, 1965. Eight days before Johnson's speech, a series of dramatic confrontations unfolded in Selma, Alabama, where civil rights activists had organized a march to Montgomery to publicize voting rights discrimination and demand legal reform. The event received national media attention after police officers wielding night sticks and tear gas attacked marchers. Public outrage intensified when, two days later, a white civil rights activist was beaten to death. In his speech before Congress, excerpted here, Johnson refers to this racial violence, adopting the phrase "we shall overcome" in his impassioned plea for voting rights, a powerful weapon in the fight against racism.

Excerpted from Lyndon B. Johnson's address before the United States Congress, Washington, DC, March 15, 1965.

I speak tonight for the dignity of man and the destiny of Democracy. I urge every member of both parties, Americans of all religions and of all colors, from every section of this country, to join me in that cause.

At times, history and fate meet at a single time in a single place to shape a turning point in man's unending search for freedom. So it was at Lexington and Concord. So it was a century ago at Appomattox. So it was last week in Selma, Alabama. There, long suffering men and women peacefully protested the denial of their rights as Americans. Many of them were brutally assaulted. One good man—a man of God—was killed.

There is no cause for pride in what has happened in Selma. There is no cause for self-satisfaction in the long denial of equal rights of millions of Americans. But there is cause for hope and for faith in our Democracy in what is happening here tonight. For the cries of pain and the hymns and protests of oppressed people have summoned into convocation all the majesty of this great government—the government of the greatest nation on earth. Our mission is at once the oldest and the most basic of this country—to right wrong, to do justice, to serve man. In our time we have come to live with the moments of great crises. Our lives have been marked with debate about great issues, issues of war and peace, issues of prosperity and depression.

But rarely in any time does an issue lay bare the secret heart of America itself. Rarely are we met with a challenge, not to our growth or abundance, or our welfare or our security, but rather to the values and the purposes and the meaning of our beloved nation. The issue of equal rights for American Negroes is such an issue. And should we defeat every enemy, and should we double our wealth and conquer the stars, and still be unequal to this issue, then we will have failed as a people and as a nation. For, with a country as with a person, "what is a man profited if he shall gain the whole world, and lose his own soul?"

There is no Negro problem. There is no Southern problem. There is no Northern problem. There is only an American problem.

And we are met here tonight as Americans—not as Democrats or Republicans; we're met here as Americans to solve that problem. This was the first nation in the history of the world to be founded with a purpose.

America's Promise

The great phrases of that purpose still sound in every American heart, North and South: "All men are created equal." "Government by consent of the governed." "Give me liberty or give me death." And those are not just clever words, and those are not just empty theories. In their name Americans have fought and died for two centuries and tonight around the world they stand there as guardians of our liberty risking their lives. Those words are promised to every citizen that he shall share in the dignity of man. This dignity cannot be found in a man's possessions. It cannot be found in his power or in his position. It really rests on his right to be treated as a man equal in opportunity to all others. It says that he shall share in freedom. He shall choose his leaders, educate his children, provide for his family according to his ability and his merits as a human being.

To apply any other test, to deny a man his hopes because of his color or race or his religion or the place of his birth is not only to do injustice, it is to deny Americans and to dishonor the dead who gave their lives for American freedom. Our fathers believed that if this noble view of the rights of man was to flourish it must be rooted in democracy. This most basic right of all was the right to choose your own leaders. The history of this country in large measure is the history of expansion of the right to all of our people.

Many of the issues of civil rights are very complex and most difficult. But about this there can and should be no argument: every American citizen must have an equal right to vote. There is no reason which can excuse the denial of that right. There is no duty which weighs more heavily on us than the duty we have to insure that right. Yet the harsh fact is that in many places in this country men and women are kept from voting simply because they are Negroes.

Every device of which human ingenuity is capable, has been used to deny this right. The Negro citizen may go to register only to be told that the day is wrong, or the hour is late, or the official in charge is absent. And if he persists and, if he manages to present himself to the registrar, he may be disqualified because he did not spell out his middle name, or because he abbreviated a word on the application. And if he manages to fill out an application, he is given a test. The registrar is the sole judge of whether he passes this test. He may be asked to recite the entire Constitution, or explain the most complex provisions of state law.

And even a college degree cannot be used to prove that he can read and write. For the fact is that the only way to pass these barriers is to show a white skin. Experience has clearly shown that the existing process of law cannot overcome systematic and ingenious discrimination. No law that we now have on the books, and I have helped to put three of them there, can insure the right to vote when local officials are determined to deny it. In such a case, our duty must be clear to all of us. The Constitution says that no person shall be kept from voting because of his race or his color.

We have all sworn an oath before God to support and to defend that Constitution. We must now act in obedience to that oath. Wednesday, I will send to Congress a law designed to eliminate illegal barriers to the right to vote. The broad principles of that bill will be in the hands of the Democratic and Republican leaders tomorrow. After they have reviewed it, it will come here formally as a bill. I am grateful for this opportunity to come here tonight at the invitation of the leadership to reason with my friends, to give them my views and to visit with my former colleagues.

I have had prepared a more comprehensive analysis of the legislation which I had intended to transmit to the clerk tomorrow, but which I will submit to the clerks tonight. But I want to really discuss the main proposals of this legislation. This bill will strike down restrictions to voting in all elections, federal, state and local, which have been used to deny Negroes the right to vote.

This bill will establish a simple, uniform standard which cannot be used, however ingenious the effort, to flout our Constitution. It will provide for citizens to be registered by officials of the United States Government, if the state officials refuse to register them. It will eliminate tedious, unnecessary lawsuits which delay the right to vote. Finally, this legislation will insure that properly registered individuals are not prohibited from voting. I will welcome the suggestions from all the members of Congress—I have no doubt that I will get some—on ways and means to strengthen this law and to make it effective.

Open the Polls

But experience has plainly shown that this is the only path to carry out the command of the Constitution. To those who seek to avoid action by their national government in their home communities, who want to and who seek to maintain purely local control over elections, the answer is simple: open your polling places to all your people. Allow men and women to register and vote whatever the color of their skin. Extend the rights of citizenship to every citizen of this land. There is no Constitutional issue here. The command of the Constitution is plain. There is no moral issue. It is wrong—deadly wrong—to deny any of your fellow Americans the right to vote in this country.

There is no issue of state's rights or national rights. There is only the struggle for human rights. I have not the slightest doubt what will be your answer. But the last time a President sent a civil rights bill to the Congress it contained a provision to protect voting rights in Federal elections. That civil rights bill was passed after eight long months of debate. And when that bill came to my desk from the Congress for signature, the heart of the voting provision had been eliminated.

This time, on this issue, there must be no delay, or no hesitation, or no compromise with our purpose. We cannot, we must not, refuse to protect the right of every American to vote in every election that he may desire to participate in.

And we ought not, and we cannot, and we must not wait another eight months before we get a bill. We have already waited 100 years and more and the time for waiting is gone. So I ask you to join me in working long hours and nights and weekends, if necessary, to pass this bill. And I don't make that request lightly, for, from the window where I sit, with the problems of our country, I recognize that from outside this chamber is the outraged conscience of a nation, the grave concern of many nations and the harsh judgment of history on our acts.

But even if we pass this bill the battle will not be over. What happened in Selma is part of a far larger movement which reaches into every section and state of America. It is the effort of American Negroes to secure for themselves the full blessings of American life. Their cause must be our cause too. Because it's not just Negroes, but really it's all of us, who must overcome the crippling legacy of bigotry and injustice.

And we shall overcome.

As a man whose roots go deeply into Southern soil, I know how agonizing racial feelings are. I know how difficult it is to reshape the attitudes and the structure of our society. But a century has passed—more than 100 years—since the Negro was freed. And he is not fully free tonight. It was more than 100 years ago that Abraham Lincoln—a great President of another party—signed the Emancipation Proclamation. But emancipation is a proclamation and not a fact.

A century has passed—more than 100 years—since equality was promised, and yet the Negro is not equal. A century has passed since the day of promise, and the promise is unkept. The time of justice has now come, and I tell you that I believe sincerely that no force can hold it back. It is right in the eyes of man and God that it should come, and when it does, I think that day will brighten the lives of every American. For Negroes are not the only victims. How many white children have gone uneducated? How many white families have lived in stark poverty? How many white lives have been scarred by fear, because we wasted energy and our substance to maintain the barriers of hatred and terror?

And so I say to all of you here and to all in the nation tonight that those who appeal to you to hold on to the past do so at the cost of denying you your future. This great rich, restless country can offer opportunity and education and hope to all—all, black and white, North and South, sharecropper and city dweller. These are the enemies: poverty, ignorance, disease. They are our enemies, not our fellow man, not our neighbor.

And these enemies too—poverty, disease and ignorance—we shall overcome.

Now let none of us in any section look with prideful righteousness on the troubles in another section or the problems of our neighbors. There is really no part of America where the promise of equality has been fully kept. In Buffalo as well as in Birmingham, in Philadelphia as well as Selma, Americans are struggling for the fruits of freedom.

This is one nation. What happens in Selma and Cincinnati is a matter of legitimate concern to every American. But let each of us look within our own hearts and our own communities and let each of us put our shoulder to the wheel to root out injustice wherever it exists. As we meet here in this peaceful historic chamber tonight, men from the South, some of whom were at Iwo Jima, men from the North who have carried Old Glory to the far corners of the world and who brought it back without a stain on it, men from the east and from the west are all fighting together without regard to religion or color or region in Vietnam.

Men from every region fought for us across the world 20 years ago. And now in these common dangers, in these common sacrifices, the South made its contribution of honor and gallantry no less than any other region in the great republic.

And in some instances, a great many of them, more. And I have not the slightest doubt that good men from everywhere in this country, from the Great Lakes to the Gulf of Mexico, from the Golden Gate to the harbors along the Atlantic, will rally now together in this cause to vindicate the freedom of all Americans. For all of us owe this duty and I believe that all of us will respond to it.

Your president makes that request of every American.

The real hero of this struggle is the American Negro. His actions and protests, his courage to risk safety, and even to risk his life, have awakened the conscience of this nation. His demonstrations have been designed to call attention to injustice, designed to provoke change; designed to stir reform. He has been called upon to make good the promise of America.

And who among us can say that we would have made the same progress were it not for his persistent bravery and his faith in American democracy?

Black Power

Stokely Carmichael

A fiery and passionate speaker, Stokely Carmichael established himself as one of the most articulate spokespersons for black militancy during the civil rights movement. Carmichael launched his career as an activist while attending college at Howard University, most notably participating in several Freedom Rides, interracial bus trips organized to challenge segregation in public transportation. Carmichael went on to become chairman of the Student Nonviolent Coordinating Committee (SNCC). As leader of the SNCC, Carmichael led the organization to harden its moderate stance on race relations and reject Martin Luther King's policy of nonviolence and integration.

During a march in June 1966, Carmichael gave a speech in which he used the term *black power*. Although the term was not new—Richard Wright had used it in reference to colonialists in Africa—it became somewhat of a battle cry for black militants in America. In a 1966 speech at the University of California in Berkeley, excerpted here, Carmichael describes black power as a means of wielding group power and explains why the term generates fear and suspicion in the white community. Arguing that blacks must achieve self-determination, Carmichael demands that whites tear down racism in their own community and institutions.

T he institutions that function in this country are clearly racist; they're built upon racism. The questions to be dealt with then are: How can black people inside this country move? How can white people who say they're not part of those institutions begin to move? And how then do we begin to clear away the obstacles that we have in this society, to make us live like human beings?

Several people have been upset because we've said that integration was irrelevant when initiated by blacks, and that in fact it was an insidious subterfuge for the maintenance of white supremacy. In the past six years or so, this country has been feeding us a "thalidomide drug [a drug that was found to have very harmful effects on human development] of integration," and some Negroes have been walking down a dream street talking about sitting next to white people. That does not begin to solve the problem. We didn't go to Mississippi to sit next to Ross Barnett [former Governor of Mississippi], we did not go to sit next to Jim Clark [sheriff of Selma, Alabama], we went to get them out of our way. People ought to understand that; we were never fighting for the right to integrate, *we were fighting against white supremacy.* In order to understand white supremacy we must dismiss the fallacious notion that white people can give anybody his freedom. A man is born free. You may enslave a man after he is born free, and that is in fact what this country does. It enslaves blacks after they're born. The only thing white people can do *is stop denying black people their freedom.*

I maintain that every civil rights bill in this country was passed for white people, not for black people. For example, I am black. I know that. I also know that while I am black I am a human being. Therefore I have the right to go into any public place. White people didn't know that. Every time I tried to go into a public place they stopped me. So some boys had to write a bill to tell that white man, "He's a human being; don't stop him." That bill was for the white man, not for me. I knew I could vote all the time and that it wasn't a privilege but my right. Every time I tried I was shot, killed or jailed, beaten or economically deprived. So somebody had to write a bill to tell white people, "When a black man comes to vote, don't bother him." That bill was for white people. I know I can live anyplace I want to live. It is white people across this country who are incapable of allowing me to live where I want. You need a civil rights bill, not me. The failure of the civil rights bill isn't because of Black Power or because

of the Student Nonviolent Coordinating Committee or because of the rebellions that are occurring in the major cities.
That failure is due to the whites' incapacity to deal with their
own problems inside their own communities.

And so in a sense we must ask, How is it that black
people move? And what do we do? But the question in a
much greater sense is, How can white people who are the
majority, and who are responsible for making democracy
work, make it work? They have failed miserably on this
point. They have never made democracy work, be it inside
the United States, Vietnam, South Africa, the Philippines,
South America, Puerto Rico, or wherever America has been.
We not only condemn the country for what it has done in-
ternally, but we must condemn it for what it does externally.
We see this country trying to rule the world, and someone
must stand up and start articulating that this country is not
God, and that it cannot rule the world.

The white supremacist attitude, which you have either
consciously or subconsciously, is running rampant through
society today. For example, missionaries were sent to Africa
with the attitude that blacks were automatically inferior. As
a matter of fact, the first act the missionaries did when they
got to Africa was to make us cover up our bodies, because
they said it got them excited. We couldn't go bare-breasted
anymore because they got excited! When the missionaries
came to civilize us because we were uncivilized, to educate us
because we were uneducated, and to give us some literate
studies because we were illiterate, they charged a price. The
missionaries came with the Bible, and we had the land; when
they left, they had the land, and we still have the Bible. That's
been the rationalization for Western civilization as it moves
across the world—stealing, plundering and raping everybody
in its path. Their one rationalization is that the rest of the
world is uncivilized and they are in fact civilized. But the
West is un-civ-i-lized. And that still runs on today, you see,
because now we have "modern-day missionaries," and they
come into our ghettos—they Head Start, Upward Lift, Boot-
strap, and Upward Bound us into white society. They don't
want to face the real problem. A man is poor for one reason
and one reason only—he does not have money. If you want

to get rid of poverty, you give people money. And you ought not to tell me about people who don't work, and that you can't give people money if they don't work, because if that were true, you'd have to start stopping Rockefeller, Kennedy, Lyndon Baines Johnson, Lady Bird Johnson, the whole of Standard Oil, the Gulf Corporation, all of them, including probably a large number of the board of trustees of this university. The question, then, is not whether or not one can work; it's *Who has power to make his or her acts legitimate?* That is all. In this country that power is invested in the hands of white people, and it makes their acts legitimate.

Black Power

We are now engaged in a psychological struggle in this country about whether or not black people have the right to use the words they want to use without white people giving their sanction. We maintain the use of the words Black Power—let them address themselves to that. We are not going to wait for white people to sanction Black Power. We're tired of waiting; every time black people try to move in this country, they're forced to defend their position beforehand. It's time that white people do that. They ought to start defending themselves as to why they have oppressed and exploited us. A man was picked as a slave for one reason—the color of his skin. Black was automatically inferior, inhuman, and therefore fit for slavery, so the question of whether or not we are individually suppressed is nonsensical, and it's a downright lie. We are oppressed as a group because we are black, not because we are lazy or apathetic, not because we're stupid or we stink, not because we eat watermelon or have good rhythm. We are oppressed because we are black.

In order to escape that oppression we must wield the group power we have, not the individual power that this country sets as the criterion under which a man may come into it. That's what is called integration. "You do what I tell you to do and we'll let you sit at the table with us." Well, if you believe in integration, you can come live in Watts, send your children to the ghetto schools. Let's talk about that. If you believe in integration, then we're going to start adopting us some white people to live in our neighborhoods. So it is clear that this question is not one of integration or segregation. We cannot afford to be concerned about the 6 per cent of black children in this country whom you allow to enter white schools. We are going to be concerned about the 94 per cent. You ought to be concerned about them too. But are we willing to be concerned about the black people who will never get to Berkeley, never get to Harvard, and cannot get an education, the ones you'll never get a chance to rub shoulders with and say, "Why, he's almost as good as we are; he's not like the others"? The question is, How can white society begin to move to see black people as human beings? I am black, therefore I am. Not: I am black and I must go to college to prove myself. I am black, therefore I am. And don't deprive me of anything and say to me that you must go to college before you gain access to X, Y, and Z. That's only a rationalization for suppression.

Antiracist Political Institutions

The political parties of this country do not meet the needs of the people on a day-to-day basis. How can we build new political institutions that will become the political expressions of people? How can you build political institutions that will begin to meet the needs of Oakland, California? The need of Oakland, California, is not 1,000 policemen with submachine guns. They need that least of all. How can we build institutions that will allow those people to function on a day-to-day basis, so that they can get decent jobs and have decent houses, and they can begin to participate in the policy and make the decisions that affect their lives? That's what they need, not Gestapo troops, because this is not 1942, and if you play like Nazis, we're not going to play Jew this time around. Get hip to that. Can white people move inside their own community and start tearing down racism where in fact it exists? It is you who live in Cicero and stopped us from living there. White people stopped us from moving into Grenada, Miss. White people make sure that we live in the ghettos of this country. White institutions do that. They must change. In order for America to really live on a basic principle of human relationships, a new society must be born. Racism must die. The economic exploitation by this country of non-white people around the world must also die.

There are several programs in the South where whites are trying to organize poor whites so they can begin to move around the question of economic exploitation and political disfranchisement. We've all heard the theory several times. But few people are willing to go into it. The question is, Can the white activist stop trying to be a Pepsi generation who comes alive in the black community, and be a man who's willing to move into the white community and start organizing where the organization is needed? Can he do that? Can the white activist disassociate himself from the clowns who waste time parrying with each other and start talking about the problems that are facing people in this state? You must start inside the white community. Our political position is that we don't think the Democratic Party represents the needs of black people. We know that it does not. If, in fact, white people believe that they're going to move inside that structure, how are they going to organize around a concept of whiteness based on true brotherhood and on stopping economic exploitation in order to form a coalition base for black people to hook up with? You cannot build a coalition based on national sentiment. If you want a coalition to address itself to real changes in this country, white people must start building those institutions inside the white community. And that's the real question facing the white activists today. Can they tear down the institutions that have put us all in the trick bag we've been into for the last hundreds of years? Frederick Douglass said that the youth should fight to be leaders today. God knows we need to be leaders today, because the men who run this country are sick. We must begin to start building those institutions and to fight to articulate our position, to fight to be able to control our universities (we need to be able to do that), to fight to control the basic institutions that perpetuate racism by destroying them and building new ones. That's the real question that faces us today, and it is a dilemma because most of us don't know how to work.

Most white activists run into the black community as an excuse. We cannot have white people working in the black community—on psychological grounds. The fact is that all black people question whether or not they are equal to whites, since every time they start to do something, white people are around showing them how to do it. If we are going to eliminate that for the generation that comes after us, then black people must be in positions of power, doing and articulating for themselves. That's not reverse racism; it is moving onto healthy ground; it is becoming what the philosopher Sartre says, an "antiracist racist." And this country can't understand that. What we have in SNCC is antiracist racism. We are against racists. If everybody who's white sees himself as racist and sees us against him, he's speaking from his own guilt. . . .

Calculated Poverty

This country assumes that if someone is poor, they are poor because of their own individual blight, or because they weren't born on the right side of town, or they had too many children, or went in the army too early, or because their father was a drunk, or they didn't care about school—they made a mistake. That's a lot of nonsense. Poverty is well calculated in this country, and the reason why the poverty program won't work is because the calculators of poverty are administering it.

   How can you, as the youth in this country, move to start carrying those things out? Move into the white community. We have developed a movement in the black community. The white activist has miserably failed to develop the movement inside of his community. Will white people have the courage to go into white communities and start organizing them? That's the question for the white activist. We won't get caught up in questions about power. This country knows what power is. It knows what Black Power is because it deprived black people of it for over four hundred years. White people associate Black Power with violence because of their own inabilty to deal with blackness. If we had said "Negro power" nobody would get scared. Everybody would support it. If we said power for colored people, everybody'd be for that, but it is the word "black" that bothers people in this country, and that's their problem, not mine. That's the lie that says anything black is bad. . . .

We must wage a psychological battle on the right for black people to define themselves as they see fit, and organize themselves as they see fit. We don't know whether the white community will allow for that organizing, because once they do they must also allow for the organizing inside their own community. It doesn't make a difference, though—we're going to organize our way. The question is how we're going to facilitate those matters, whether it's going to be done with a thousand policemen with submachine guns, or whether it's going to be done in a context where it's allowed by white people warding off those policemen. Are white people who call themselves activists ready to move into the white communities on two counts, on building new political institutions to destroy the old ones that we have, and to move around the concept of white youth refusing to go into the army? If so, then we can start to build a new world. We must urge you to fight now to be the leaders of today, not tomorrow. This country is a nation of thieves. It stands on the brink of becoming a nation of murderers. We must stop it. We must stop it. We must stop it.

We are on the move for our liberation. We're tired of trying to prove things to white people. We are tired of trying to explain to white people that we're not going to hurt them. We are concerned with getting the things we want, the things we have to have to be able to function. The question is, Will white people overcome their racism and allow for that to happen in this country? If not, we have no choice but to say very clearly, "Move on over, or we're going to move on over you."

GREAT
SPEECHES
IN
HISTORY

The Fight
for Rights
Continues

Our Time Has Come

Jesse Jackson

By the 1980s, Jesse Jackson had become perhaps the most prominent advocate for civil rights issues in the United States. While in college in the early 1960s, Jackson began his career as a black activist when he was named field director of the Congress of Racial Equality (CORE) and, in 1966, was appointed by Martin Luther King Jr. to organize Operation Breadbasket, which sought to fight racial discrimination in the North. In 1971 Jackson founded Operation PUSH (People United to Save Humanity) to create equal economic opportunities for blacks.

In 1984 Jackson launched a campaign for the Democratic presidential nomination, gaining the support of a considerable number of white as well as black voters. He solicited an even broader following through his diverse "rainbow coalition" of Hispanics, Asians, disadvantaged whites, and other minority groups. Jackson's address to the Democratic National Convention in 1984, excerpted here, sets forth the goals of his campaign. Although he did not win the party's nomination, Jackson's campaign was the launching pad for a stronger—albeit ultimately unsuccessful—bid for the nomination four years later.

Tonight we come together bound by our faith in a mighty God, with genuine respect and love for our country, and inheriting the legacy of a great party, the Democratic Party, which is the best hope for redirecting our

Excerpted from Jesse Jackson's speech before the Democratic National Convention, July 18, 1984.

nation on a more humane, just and peaceful course.

This is not a perfect party. We are not a perfect people. Yet, we are called to a perfect mission: our mission to feed the hungry; to clothe the naked; to house the homeless; to teach the illiterate; to provide jobs for the jobless; and to choose the human race over the nuclear race.

We are gathered here this week to nominate a candidate and adopt a platform which will expand, unify, direct and inspire our Party and the Nation to fulfill this mission.

My constituency is the desperate, the damned, the disinherited, the disrespected, and the despised. They are restless and seek relief. They've voted in record numbers. They have invested faith, hope and trust that they have in us. The Democratic Party must send them a signal that we care. I pledge my best to not let them down.

There is the call of conscience, redemption, expansion, healing and unity. Leadership must heed the call of conscience, redemption, expansion, healing and unity, for they are the key to achieving our mission. Time is neutral and does not change things. With courage and initiative, leaders can change things.

No generation can choose the age or circumstance in which it is born, but through leadership it can choose to make the age in which it is born, an age of enlightenment, an age of jobs and peace and justice. . . .

The Rainbow Coalition

Our flag is red, white and blue, but our nation is a rainbow—red, yellow, brown, black and white—and we're all precious in God's sight.

America is not like a blanket—one piece of unbroken cloth, the same color, the same texture, the same size. America is more like a quilt—many patches, many pieces, many colors, many sizes, all woven and held together by a common thread. The white, the Hispanic, the black, the Arab, the Jew, the woman, the Native American, the small farmer, the business person, the environmentalist, the peace activist, the young, the old, the lesbian, the gay and the disabled make up the American quilt.

Even in our fractured state, all of us count and all of us fit somewhere. We have proven that we can survive without each other. But we have not proven that we can win and progress without each other. We must come together.

From Fannie Lou Hamer in Atlantic City in 1964 to the Rainbow Coalition in San Francisco today; from the Atlantic to the Pacific, we have experienced pain but progress as we ended American apartheid laws, we got public accommodation, we secured voting rights, we obtained open housing, as young people got the right to vote. We lost Malcolm, Martin, Medgar, Bobby, John and Viola. The team that got us here must be expanded, not abandoned.

Twenty years ago, tears welled up in our eyes as the bodies of Schwerner, Goodman and Chaney were dredged from the depths of a river in Mississippi. Twenty years later, our communities, black and Jewish, are in anguish, anger and pain. Feelings have been hurt on both sides.

There is a crisis in communications. Confusion is in the air. But we cannot afford to lose our way. We may agree to agree; or agree to disagree on issues; we must bring back civility to these tensions.

We are co-partners in a long and rich religious history— the Judeo-Christian traditions. Many blacks and Jews have a shared passion for social justice at home and peace abroad. We must seek a revival of the spirit, inspired by a new vision and new possibilities. We must return to higher ground.

We are bound by Moses and Jesus, but also connected with Islam and Mohammed. These three great religions, Judaism, Christianity and Islam, were all born in the revered and holy city of Jerusalem.

We are bound by Dr. Martin Luther King Jr. and Rabbi Abraham Heschel, crying out from their graves for us to reach common ground. We are bound by shared blood and shared sacrifices. We are much too intelligent; much too bound by our Judeo-Christian heritage; much too victimized by racism, sexism, militarism and anti-Semitism; much too threatened as historical scapegoats to go on divided one from another. We must turn from finger pointing to clasped hands. We must share our burdens and our joys with each other once again. We must turn to each other and not on each other and choose higher ground.

Twenty years later, we cannot be satisfied by just restoring the old coalition. Old wine skins must make room for new wine. We must heal and expand. The Rainbow Coalition is making room for Arab Americans. They, too, know the pain and hurt of racial and religious rejection. They must not continue to be made pariahs. The Rainbow Coalition is making room for Hispanic Americans who this very night are living under the threat of the Simpson-Mazzoli bill. And farm workers from Ohio who are fighting the Campbell Soup Company with a boycott to achieve legitimate workers' rights.

The Rainbow is making room for the Native American, the most exploited people of all, a people with the greatest moral claim amongst us. We support them as they seek the restoration of their ancient land and claim amongst us. We support them as they seek the restoration of land and water rights, as they seek to preserve their ancestral homelands and the beauty of a land that was once all theirs. They can never receive a fair share for all they have given us. They must finally have a fair chance to develop their great resources and to preserve their people and their culture.

The Rainbow Coalition includes Asian Americans, now being killed in our streets, scapegoats for the failures of corporate, industrial and economic policies.

The Rainbow is making room for the young Americans. Twenty years ago, our young people were dying in a war for which they could not even vote. Twenty years later, young America has the power to stop a war in Central America and the responsibility to vote in great numbers. Young America must be politically active in 1984. The choice is war or peace. We must make room for young America.

The Rainbow includes disabled veterans. The color scheme fits in the Rainbow. The disabled have their handicap revealed and their genius concealed; while the able-bodied have their genius revealed and their disability concealed. But ultimately, we must judge people by their values and their contribution. Don't leave anybody out. I would rather have Roosevelt in a wheelchair than Reagan on a horse.

The Rainbow includes for small farmers. They have suffered tremendously under the Reagan regime. They will either receive 90 percent parity or 100 percent charity. We must address their concerns and make room for them.

The Rainbow includes lesbians and gays. No American citizen ought to be denied equal protection from the law.

We must be unusually committed and caring as we expand our family to include new members. All of us must be tolerant and understanding as the fears and anxieties of the rejected and of the party leadership express themselves in so many different ways. Too often what we call hate—as if it were something deeply rooted in philosophy or strategy—it is simply ignorance, anxiety, paranoia, fear and insecurity.

To be strong leaders, we must be long-suffering as we seek to right the wrongs of our Party and our Nation. We must expand our Party, heal our Party and unify our Party. That is our mission in 1984.

We are often reminded that we live in a great nation— and we do. But it can be greater still. The Rainbow is mandating a new definition of greatness. We must not measure greatness from the mansion down, but from the manger up.

Jesus said that we should not be judged by the bark we wear but by the fruit that we bear. Jesus said that we must measure greatness by how we treat the least of these. . . .

Rebuilding America

In 1984, my heart is made to feel glad because I know there is a way out—justice. The requirement for rebuilding America is justice. The linchpin of progressive politics in our nation will not come from the North, they in fact will come from the South.

That is why I argue over and over again. We look from Virginia around to Texas, there's only one black Congressperson out of 115. Nineteen years later, we're locked out of the Congress, the Senate and the Governor's mansion.

What does this large black vote mean? Why do I fight to win second primaries and fight gerrymandering and annexation and at-large elections? Why do we fight over that? Because I tell you, you cannot hold someone in the ditch unless you linger there with them. Unless you linger there.

If you want a change in this nation, you enforce that voting rights act. We'll get 12 to 20 black, Hispanics, female and progressive congresspersons from the South. We can save the cotton, but we have got to fight the boll weevils. We have got to make a judgment. We have got to make a judgment.

It is not enough to hope that ERA [Equal Rights Amendment] will pass. How can we pass ERA? If blacks vote in great numbers, progressive whites win. It is the only way progressive whites win. If blacks vote in great numbers, Hispanics win. When blacks, Hispanics and progressive whites vote, women win. When women win, children win. When women and children win, workers win. We must all come together. We must come together. . . .

A Challenge to Young America

I have a message for our youth. I challenge them to put hope in their brains and not dope in their veins. I told them that like Jesus, I, too, was born in the slum, and just because you're born in a slum does not mean the slum is born in you and you can rise above it if your mind is made up. I told them in every slum there are two sides. When I see a broken window that's the slummy side. Train some youth to become a glazier; that is the sunny side. When I see a missing brick, that is the slummy side. Let that child in a union and become a brick mason and build; that is the sunny side. When I see a missing door, that is the slummy side. Train some youth to become a carpenter, that is the sunny side. When I see the vulgar words and hieroglyphics of destitution on the walls, that is the slummy side. Train some youth to be a painter and artist, that is the sunny side.

We leave this place looking for the sunny side because there's a brighter side somewhere. I am more convinced than ever that we can win. We will vault up the rough side of the mountain. We can win. I just want young America to do me one favor, just one favor.

Exercise the right to dream. You must face reality, that which is. But then dream of a reality that ought to be, that must be. Live beyond the pain of reality with the dream of a bright tomorrow. Use hope and imagination as weapons of survival and progress. Use love to motivate you and obligate you to serve the human family.

Young America, dream. Choose the human race over the nuclear race. Bury the weapons and don't burn the people. Dream—dream of a new value system. Teachers who teach for life and not just for a living; teach because they can't help it. Dream of lawyers more concerned about justice than a judgeship. Dream of doctors more concerned about public health than personal wealth. Dream of preachers and priests who will prophesy and not just profiteer. Preach and dream! Our time has come. Our time has come.

Suffering breeds character. Character breeds faith, and in the end faith will not disappoint. Our time has come. Our faith, hope and dreams have prevailed. Our time has come. Weeping has endured for nights but that joy cometh in the morning.

Our time has come. No grave can hold our body down. Our time has come. No lie can live forever. Our time has come. We must leave the racial battle ground and come to the economic common ground and moral higher ground. America, our time has come.

We come from disgrace to amazing grace. Our time has come. Give me your tired, give me your poor, your huddled masses who yearn to breathe free and come November, there will be a change because our time has come.

Thank you and God bless you.

Apartheid and the American Civil Rights Movement

Nelson Mandela

In the latter half of the twentieth century, Nelson Mandela led the struggle to end apartheid, South Africa's brutal regime that for decades denied blacks basic human rights through the legal separation of the races. Jailed as a political prisoner for twenty-seven years, Mandela garnered worldwide support against apartheid and became a symbol to all disadvantaged people seeking freedom and self-determination.

Shortly after his release from prison in 1990, Mandela toured the United States, stopping in Atlanta, Georgia, to speak at a mass rally at the Georgia Institute of Technology. In his address, reprinted here, Mandela compares the American civil rights movement to South Africa's struggles to create a racially integrated society. Mandela went on to become the African National Congress (ANC) president in 1994 and played a pivotal role in ending apartheid.

I am happy to bring you warm and fraternal greetings from the ANC [African National Congress], the mass democratic movement, and the fighting people of South Africa. . . .

I am doubly happy to be in Atlanta. Atlanta which is the hometown of Dr. Martin Luther King, Jr. And the scene of

---

Excerpted from Nelson Mandela's speech to the Georgia Institute of Technology, Atlanta, Georgia, 1990.

many civil rights battles. We are also conscious of the fact that in the southern part of this country you have experienced the degradation and inhumanity of slavery and racial discrimination as well as the lynchings and brutal intimidation from those men in white robes. We continue to be inspired by the knowledge that in the face of your own awesome difficulties you are in the forefront of the anti-apartheid movement in this country. Your principled stand demonstrates clearly to us that we are in the midst of fellow freedom fighters, that here we have powerful fighters against racism wherever and whenever it rears its evil head.

"Let Freedom Ring"

The extraordinary reception accorded to us by the people of New York, Boston, Washington, and Atlanta fills us with joy and gives us added strength for the coming battles. I am honored by your presence in the city that gave the world a Dr. Martin Luther King, a giant among giants. Dr. King lit up the firmament of struggle against racism, injustice, poverty, and war. In our prison cells, we felt a kinship and affinity with him and were inspired by his indomitable fighting spirit. Even now, twenty-seven years later, I am deeply moved by his outstanding speech at the mammoth march in Washington in 1963. With passion, sincerity, and brilliant eloquence he declared, I quote, "I have a dream that one day on the red hills of Georgia the sons of former slaves and the sons of former slave owners will be able to sit down together at the table of brotherhood. I have a dream that one day even the state of Mississippi, a state sweltering with the heat of injustice, sweltering with the heat of oppression, will be transformed into an oasis of freedom and justice," unquote. As the fervor and applause of the crowd reached a crescendo, Dr. King exclaimed, quote, "Let freedom ring," unquote. Let us all exclaim, Let freedom ring in South Africa. Let freedom ring wherever the people's human rights are trampled upon, let freedom ring.

Dr. King's dreams are now becoming the stuff of reality. At the time he began his anti-racist civil rights crusade there were only 300 elected black officials. Today it fills me with pride to know that there are nearly 6,000 black elected officials in this country. His dreams are suddenly going to see the light of day in our country as well. Dr. King also has the distinction of being the first black American to put the issue of apartheid racism into the middle of the American political agenda. Dr. King rightly deserved the Nobel Peace Prize. We are of course proud that two of our sons, Chief Albert Luthuli and Archbishop Desmond Tutu, were similarly honored. Chief Luthuli was a patient, humble, kind, warm, and compassionate person. He was a brilliant thinker and political strategist. Under his leadership the ANC emerged as a powerful, united, and disciplined mass organization. Both these great freedom fighters were men of honor and noble dignity. Of them we can say the man died but his memory lives. The man died but his fighting spirit imbues us all. The man died but his ideas and ideals live. Allow me to express our best wishes to Mrs. Coretta Scott King.

Brothers and sisters, as you know, apartheid South Africa is skilled in imparity. The unrelenting racist tyranny and the destructive fury of war unleashed on peoples of our region has led to the death of hundreds of thousands of people and the impoverishment of millions. But our people did not flinch from doing their duty. Prisons, torture, and even death could not and never will cow us into submission. We will never acquiesce in our own oppression. We will never surrender. We will pursue the struggle until we have transformed South Africa into a united, nonracial, nonsexist democratic country.

Our people who have shed the rivers of blood need democracy; all our people, black and white, need democracy. We are engaged in a life-and-death struggle to bring into being a future in which all shall, without regard to race, color, creed or sex have the right to vote and to be voted into all elected organs of the state.

Sisters and brothers, we are on the brink of major changes in South Africa. Victory is in sight. But before we reach that promised land we still have to travel a torturous road. Apartheid is still in place. Apartheid continues to imprison, brutalize, maim, and kill our people. Apartheid continues to destroy the future of our children. Apartheid remains a crime against humanity. In this context we say that sanctions must be maintained. We appeal to you, keep the pressure on apartheid. Keep the pressure on apartheid.

Apartheid Must Go

I am happy to report that we had warm, friendly, and fruitful meetings with President [George] Bush and Secretary of State Mr. [James] Baker. It was a meeting of minds on the most important issues determining the future of our country. It gives us great confidence to know that in your country there is developing a national anti-apartheid consensus. From the streets of New York, the institutions of learning in Boston, the churches of Atlanta, and the corridors of power in Washington, the message is clear and very unequivocal. Apartheid must go. It must go now!

This consensus was reached due to the hard and unceasing work of thousands of people, black and white. It is truly an anti-apartheid rainbow coalition. To all of you we say thank you. To all of you we say, we respect you, we admire you, and above all we love you. Thank you.

Our Nation Is Greater Because of Our Diversity

Morris Dees

Dedicated to fighting racial discrimination and pursuing equal opportunities for minorities, attorney Morris Dees was at the forefront of many civil rights issues in the United States by the time the twentieth century ended. As cofounder of the Southern Poverty Law Center (SPLC), a nonprofit organization that combats intolerance and discrimination through litigation and educational programs, Dees has participated in a variety of legal cases targeting hate groups and other organized racist activity. His most well-known victory secured a $12.5 million judgment against white supremacist leader Tom Metzger for his role in the beating death of a young black student in Oregon.

In the following address to students at Eureka College in Illinois, in 1999, Dees describes how hate groups and intolerance breed fear, pain, and divisiveness. In a moving narrative, Dees concludes that the divisions that separate disparate groups of people can be bridged only by a willingness to understand and appreciate how important each person is in making America a great nation.

There is a battle going on in this country—it didn't just start yesterday, but it is certainly intensifying. That's a battle over whose America is this? Whose version of our country is going to prevail into the next century when

you as young men and women are out in our community—
making a living, using the degree that you are earning at this
school. There are people that feel very strong about their version of America. They feel strong enough to fill a truck with
4,000 pounds of ammonium nitrate fertilizer, soak it with
diesel fuel, drive it up in front of a federal building, and ex-
plode it with little or no thought for the innocent men,
women, and children in that building. When Timothy Mc-
Veigh drove from the Murrah Federal Building in his car he
could not have helped but heard—and maybe even felt—that
tremendous explosion. And when he did, he thought of himself as a hero—as a good soldier, as a patriotic American insuring that he did his part to make sure that his version of
this nation prevailed.

We had a case at the Southern Poverty Law Center that I
think illustrates well this tremendous difference—this tremendous difference that we have along those divisions that separate us so much in this country. Because America is deeply divided. There are a lot of wonderful and good things about our
nation—and I'm not here to put American down, but to say
that we can be better. We are divided along lines in this country of sexual orientation, because of the tragic death of a student at the University of Wyoming recently, we are divided
along lines of gender, we are divided along lines of race and religion and ethnic differences that would cause a young man
like Ben Smith—a follower of Matthew Hale of the World
Church of the Creator—to gun down basketball coach Ricky
Byrdsong and shoot a Korean student and shoot others. We are
divided in this country also along lines of class—those people
on one side who have economic goods and wealth and power
and those that don't—and the battles are fought out over how
we are going to split up the economic pie in this nation. They
are fought out in the city councils and the county governments
of our country all the way to the halls of Congress.

But I mentioned to you a case that we had that I think illustrates these differences that separate us so much today as
you prepare to go out into the world. Our client there was a
family from Ethiopia—a very poor country in Africa—who
had sent their twenty-four-year-old son Mulugeta Seraw to
come to the United States to get an education. He left behind

his son, Henok, and his wife. Henok was about six years old. When Mulugeta boarded the plane in Addis Ababa to come to Portland Junior College to go to school in Portland, Oregon, he thought to himself, "America is a great nation—I have heard so much about America—I have heard that if you work hard, if you save your money, if you get a good education, if you stay out of trouble, you've got a good chance of getting ahead." And when he got to our country he worked hard—he had to send money back home to his wife and child and he got a job while he was a student at Avis Rent-a-Car. His job was to drive people from the airport in Portland in a van out to where Avis parked their cars. Often times people would leave an umbrella or a billfold or a briefcase or a package on his bus and he would use his own money—on many occasions—to make sure that it got shipped back to them. For his good work at Avis, he was elected employee of the month of Avis Rent-a-Car.

The White Aryan Resistance

But there was another man that had a whole different view about whose America this is and his name was Tom Metzger. You may never have heard of him—he has been on the Donahue and the Oprah show and Sally Jessie Raphael—he was from California down in Fallbrook, California, and at fifty-five having been a failed politician he set up an organization called the White Aryan Resistance (WAR). The White Aryan Resistance, under his leadership, became kind of the head organization for skinhead groups around the nation—racist skinheads who went around the streets causing trouble with minorities.

And Metzger taught his followers—he said "look, America is a great nation, but we are going to fall from our position of greatness unless we get those people out of our midst who are bringing us down"—and he called those people "mud people"—anybody that wasn't a white Aryan, like himself—Jews, Americans of African descent, Asian descent, and others. He taught that it was necessary to create racial disturbances—violence—in order to hurry along the day when there is a race war in our nation and we will run these "mud people" out of America. And in order to do this, in his own twisted way, he sent organizers around the country to organize skinhead groups to be a part of the White Aryan Resistance. He sent Dave [Mazzella], one of his organizers, up to Portland, Oregon, to meet with a group of skinheads he had heard about that existed there. Dave got to town, he met the skinheads, and he told them Metzger's philosophy and the need to go into the streets and create acts of violence in order to hurry up the day when these "mud people" would have to be forced out of America.

Well, Dave got there and he taught some skinheads his beliefs and about three weeks later, a couple of skinheads around midnight (that Dave had been talking to) walked out on the street and they saw a black man get out of a car and walk toward an apartment building. They rushed over and they taunted him—they punched him in the chest—and they called him racist names trying to provoke him to swing at them. It was Mulugeta coming home from his job at Avis, and he said "Peace, peace—please—no trouble—no trouble." And while they continued to taunt him, one of the skinheads walked around behind him and took a full swing with a baseball bat and crushed Mulugeta's skull—and he died there on the streets of Portland. The police quickly caught the skinheads that did this and they all got long prison sentences.

We got a call at the Southern Poverty Law Center from lawyers representing the family in Ethiopia saying please go out and see if you can find somebody to bring a lawsuit in a civil case. Because this little child and his mother are suffering—they need some financial help. I flew to Portland and met with the police detectives that were handling the case. They said, "Well, Mr. Dees, we understand what you want to do, but these skinheads are in prison and they have no money." And I was about to leave when one of them reached in a file drawer and pulled out a piece of paper and he said "this may help you." It was a hand-written letter to the skinheads in Portland from Metzger, and it said, "When you meet Dave, our organizer, we will teach you how we operate," signed "Tom Metzger, for a White America."

Well, I began to look for Dave. Our investigators found him. He was no longer associated with Metzger, and I met this young man and talked to him. I said, "Would you be a witness for us if we bring a suit against Metzger and his organization? Would you be a witness for us to tell that he told you to come to Portland and encourage acts of racial violence?" The young man was very sorry for what had happened—and he said that he would. We brought that lawsuit and I sent to Ethiopia and brought little Henok Seraw to come and sit at my counsel table and he listened through an interpreter to the trial. Metzger had good lawyers to represent him there, but he wanted to make his own arguments to the jury because he said, "Look, I didn't know the victim, I didn't know the skinheads; I was 1200 miles away and I have a right of free speech." He had no idea that we had Dave as a witness, because it's not free speech when you've got somebody to say you encouraged actual violence.

The Verdict

Well Dave testified, and we put on other evidence and at the close of the case Metzger stood and he said, "Ladies and gentlemen, don't find against my organization and me just because we have unpopular views—we have that right in America." And he talked on and on about his version of this country and the case and he said, "Look, I don't apologize for my views, I believe that America is a great nation because of the contributions of white people," and he sat down. I stood for a while thinking what could I say to the jury to counter that argument. I said, "Ladies and gentlemen, I want you to look at the first row of this courtroom behind Metzger's table. Those three young people sitting there—they are his children. You know not one of them had to worry about getting polio because of the genius of a Jewish doctor—Jonas Salk. And if we lived in Tom Metzger's America, we wouldn't have the brilliance of the black general Colin Powell," and I mentioned other people from other ethnic and racial backgrounds and I told the jury their contributions to the greatness of this nation. I said, "Ladies and gentlemen, the America that Tom Metzger believes in is an America that never existed. Our nation is great because of our diversity, not in spite of it." And that jury agreed with me—I think—in a

unanimous way, because they returned the largest civil ver-
dict ever returned at that time in the history of the state of
Oregon—12.5 million dollars against Metzger and the White
Aryan Resistance.

Now he didn't have 12.5 million dollars—I wish this was
the lottery—but we did take his business, his property, his
house and put him out of business—except for the few little
things he says on the media. He is no longer the leader of the
skinheads, and the skinhead movement has subsided tremendously.

You know as I was flying back to my farm in Alabama,
after being gone for nearly a year working on that case.
Thinking about all that it meant and relaxing for the first
time, when that airplane reached 30,000 feet cruising alti-
tude and I kicked back in the chair to relax, I looked out the
window as we passed over the Rocky Mountains and then finally the Great Plains that you live in, where the farms are all
there and crops in the field—and then, as I finally came in
over the Appalachian Mountains and into Atlanta I thought
to myself, "You know, I believe what I told that jury, I believe
that America is a great nation because of our diversity," but
why as we enter the next century, why can't we all get along?

These divisions that separate us in this country are causing so much hurt and pain and fear—they are ripping at the
very fabric of our democracy. Incidents pile on top of incidents—one after another—the shooting into a church, a
school, a Jewish synagogue, a day care center—one after another. There are 450 hate groups in this country operating today that we have recorded, and there may be more. There are
over 250 hate websites that are simply a click away from you
or the children of this country. What can we do? What can
you and I do to deal with this issue, because I can assure
you—you may live in a very homogeneous part of America
where most people are like you, look like you, and think like
you, but you probably won't live here during most of your
career because we are becoming very mobile as a nation.
Even here there are biases and there are prejudices that don't
always fall along racial lines but they may fall along lines of
the other divisions that I mentioned that separate us in this
country. I wish I had a simple little formula, but I think that

the bottom line—the absolute bottom line—is how we treat each other—how we act one to another in this county.

Teaching Tolerance

We have a project called Teaching Tolerance at the Southern Poverty Law Center. Seventy-seven thousand schools use Teaching Tolerance. It's free—we give away several million dollars worth of good tolerance education material annually. We teach young people in the second and third grade the hurt and pain from being singled out and identified as being different. A little child comes to school with glasses on in the second grade and comes home that night crying to mother that they had been called "little four-eyes." That might seem really funny to those kids who singled that person out and called them that, but if those students understand the pain that Suzie or Johnny felt when they came home after somebody said "We don't want Suzie on our volleyball team she's too fat, she can't run." You know what I'm talking about. Those little bits of intolerance build to big bits of intolerance that later lead to horrible, horrible hate crimes in this country.

If there is a solution to the problem that separates in this country, that divides us so, and would give you a way that you could connect the dots yourself because all of our lives are different and your life is just as different as the person sitting next to you as you begin to travel upon the roads of your future. If you could fill those dots in so that you could make a difference and that difference—I think—will make America the great nation that it is and that it can be in the future. But I think that words of a song, to me, state it best. Anybody in this audience over forty years old will know this song. It was one that we sang during the days of the Civil Rights Movement, days that we struggled with the war in Vietnam in this country, a song that was written by Peter, Paul and Mary—and sung by them. "If I Had a Hammer"—you remember—"I'd hammer in the morning, I'd hammer in the evening, and I'd hammer all over this land . . . I'd hammer out for freedom, I'd hammer out for justice, and I'd hammer out a love between our brothers and sisters"—that we can all share.

In this country we have the greatest freedom of any nation on earth—it's not perfect—the history of this school is imbued with people, men and women, educators who were seeking to make the promises written in America's Constitution real—the freedoms guaranteed in 1776—this very school was founded on those principles and you should be honored to be here. We have one of the greatest justice systems in America—and it's not perfect either—we are constantly striving to make it better and some of you may be a part of that justice system in your futures. But unless we have a love between our brothers and sisters that we can share—all the Teaching Tolerance materials and all the programs like this are really going to come to nothing.

And I'm not talking about that kind of love that you have for your family. I've got family members that I love in spite of them. We all know about families—and you know the reason I love some of my family members—I had a couple of uncles that were members of the Ku Klux Klan—one ran a little country store—because I knew them personally, and I knew the good things about them. I knew them as individuals, and I'm not talking about that kind of love you have for your girlfriend or your boyfriend or the members of your church or the people you work with—I'm talking about that love for people who are different than you are—who have different sexual orientation, who are from a different class, a different religion—or no religion, people whose skin is a different color than yours, the facial features may be different, the hair may have a different texture than yours. I'm talking about appreciating and loving people and caring about people by understanding them as human beings, and that's not easy to do because in our day-to-day life we don't come in contact with that many people who are different than we are.

And I think that an old, old black lady that I represented taught me the importance of love. Her story is a powerful one. Her son was lynched by the Ku Klux Klan in Mobile, Alabama—and this just wasn't any Klan group, it was the powerful United Klans of America whose members blew up the church in Birmingham in 1963 that killed those four little Sunday School girls. In the late 1970s and early 1980s as our country was becoming more conservative—if that's a good word, or reactionary, I think is a better word—this

Klan group was reorganizing. It had chapters in thirty states—several in Illinois—and it had a new 10,000 square foot building and money in the bank.

The Case of Michael Donald

The leaders of this Klan group sent an organizer down to Mobile, Alabama, because they had heard about a trial going on down there—a trial in which a black man was on trial for killing a white police officer. The Klan was concerned because the jury that had been chosen to hear this case was majority black. The Klan leaders told that little local Mobile, Alabama, Klan group—they said, "If that black man (and I can assure you that's not how they described him) if he gets away with killing that white police officer, we want you to go out and find a black person and we want you to kill him to set an example, that if blacks are going to sit on juries and do things that affect the whites rights of white people in America—they better be careful." They picked two young Klansmen to carry out this deed if need be—one of them was named James—his nickname was Tiger—James "Tiger" Knowles. He was seventeen and a twenty-six-year-old man named Henry Hays. They gave them a rope tied up like noose and a gun and an automobile and they all gathered to watch the jury verdict be announced on the ten o'clock news. The jury was dead-locked—and it wasn't along racial lines it later turned out—but the Klan thought this was a defeat and so they sent these two young Klansmen out to look for a black person. They drove around Mobile till close to midnight, and when on the dark street they saw a young black man walking down the street, they pulled the car over, called him over to the car, and asked him for directions to a restaurant.

They called over Michael Donald, Mrs. [Beulah Mae] Donald's only son, who was nineteen. He was coming home from his job, he worked at the Mobile Press Register in the press room—the newspaper. He was also a student at Mobile Community College. He lived alone with his mother. They asked him how do we get to a certain restaurant, and as he got near the car to give them directions, they put a gun on him and forced him into the car—carried him across the bayou bridge over into the adjacent county into the swamp and put that rope around his neck—brought him back, and hung him in a tree where his body was found the next morning at daylight in a black neighborhood. It took the police and the FBI some four years to crack that case—and only then after James "Tiger" Knowles confessed. He had gotten into some other trouble, and to help himself he confessed and told on the older Klansman. For that he got a life sentence in prison and was put in the federal witness protection program. I went to the trial in Mobile representing the Donald family because we were thinking of a civil suit—nobody had ever sued at that time (in 1986) nobody had ever sued a Klan group—or a hate group—for the acts of its members.

So I sat and watched as this young Klansman testified about the directions they got and how they went out and found Michael and what they did. After the jury—an all white jury—convicted Henry Hays and sentenced him to die, I talked to this young Klansman, James Knowles, and I said, "would you testify in a civil suit, if I brought one, against the Klan?" He said he would. We brought a suit against the Klan officials and the organization—they had money and they had property. At the trial, James "Tiger" Knowles told his story. Mrs. Donald, who had not gone to the criminal trial, came and sat at our counsel table to watch the trial. Knowles said when we got Michael in the car he begged for his life, he said, "Please, please, don't kill me—my momma depends on me." He said he jumped out of the car when he got in the woods and he tried to run, but we tackled him and we put the rope around his neck. I got this man who is now in his midtwenties to get down off the witness stand and demonstrate. He showed how he put his foot against Michael's face and he pulled on that rope with all the strength in his body while his partner had his foot against the other side of his face. I know Mrs. Donald couldn't help but see the waffled boot print still in Michael's face as I handed the autopsy photograph over to the jury.

At the end of the case the Klan lawyer asked the jury not to find his organization guilty, because it would be a bad decision to rule against an unpopular group just because of its beliefs. I told the jury that I thought that we had proved our case well. We had shown witness after witness how this group had always used violence to carry out its goals of white supremacy, and I sat down. The judge was beginning to tell the jury what their role was in the case when all of a sudden James "Tiger" Knowles leaped to his feet. He had been brought there by the United States Marshals from prison, and they jumped to their feet because they thought he was trying to escape. He turned to the judge, and he said, "Your Honor may I say something to the jury?" The judge said, "Well, you didn't have a lawyer." [I sued him because I wanted the jury to see the whole cast of characters—there was no reason to have a lawyer for him—he had nothing, but I wanted to have him sitting there with the rest of the defendants.] The judge said, "Well since you didn't have a lawyer, speak up."

Well he walked over in front of the jury and said, "Ladies and gentlemen, I've lost everything. I'll never be with my family again—I know I'll die in prison. What I did was because of racial hatred, and bigotry, and prejudice taught to me in my home and in my community." And he looked down at Mrs. Donald sitting there at my table less than ten feet away right in front of the jury and he spoke her name. His voice went quiet and I could see tears welling up in his eyes and in a few moments he was sobbing openly. I thought the judge was going to give him a chance to recover his composure with a recess, but Knowles cleared his throat, and he said, "Mrs. Donald, can you forgive me for what I did to Michael?" She kind of reared back in her chair and looked at him in front of that jury, and I'll never forget, what she said, if I live to be a hundred, she said, "Son, I've already forgiven you."

There wasn't a dry eye—I can assure you—at our counsel table, in that jury box, and I saw that old judge brush back a tear. This lady, who had lost one of the most precious things in her life, her only son, had the love between a brother and a sister that she could share. She understood pain from discrimination and prejudice—she could relate. She was a warm, intelligent, and compassionate woman, but the highest job she had ever obtained was scrubbing white folks' floors in Mobile, Alabama, as a maid. She knew what it meant to have lost opportunities for education, to own property, yet she had that love between a brother and a sister. I thought that the words that came out of her mouth that day was a higher justice than that seven million dollar verdict that jury later rendered.

The Importance of Love

I've often thought since that if we in this country had just a small bit of her mercy, understanding and compassion that those deep divisions that separate us in this country wouldn't exist. How many of us have ever looked into the face of somebody who hurt us that much and had the compassion to say I forgive you. When those divides that separate us are bridged over they are going to be bridged over by our willingness to love each other and to understand each other and appreciate how important and valuable each of us are in making this a great nation. We are going to overcome the problems that face us today. The Matthew Hales and the Ben Smiths and the Timothy McVeighs will go down in history as minor footnotes, if at all, because this nation is greater than the sum of all of those people.

At a time when America was in one of its darkest days—1963—Dr. Martin Luther King expressed his faith in this nation. He had just been let out of the Birmingham jail, the church had been blown up there and killed those four little girls, there had been no 1964 Civil Rights Act, no 1965 Voting Rights Act. There were powerful people in Congress from the South—Senators that did not intend to have equal rights for minorities, but with all of that against him, in one of the darkest hours of the Civil Rights Movement, Dr. King went to Washington to express his faith in this nation and all of its people. He stood before the Mall with a quarter of a million people there and millions watching on television and he said that "I have a dream that one day in the red clay hills of Georgia that the sons of former slaves and the sons of former slave owners will sit down around the table of brotherhood."

I think that if Dr. King was here today—and I think that if he had read about all the horrible shootings and tragedies and hate crimes we have today—and the three steps we have taken forward and the two back since his death more than thirty years ago, I think he would still have faith in America because of people like you—people of goodwill. I think if he was making that speech today I think he would say that I have a dream that one day in the red clay hills of Georgia, but today I think he would add in the barrios, in the ghettoes, on the reservations, and in the seats of economic and judicial and political power in this nation, that the sons and daughters of former slaves, and the sons and daughters of former slave owners—and today, I think he might add the homeless, the poor, the powerless, and those who hold the keys to the economic and judicial and political power of this nation will sit down around the table of person-hood and truly learn to love one another.

And I know that each of you are going to be a positive part of this great America that you are entering for the next millennium. Thank you very much.

Growing Beyond Racism

Marcia Cantarella

Marcia Cantarella is the daughter of Whitney Young, the renowned civil rights activist who headed the Urban League during the peak years of the civil rights movement. As assistant dean of Princeton University and an expert in business and public affairs, Cantarella has written and spoken on a variety of topics that affect minorities, including the empowerment of women in the workplace and entrepreneurial development.

In the following address to the Fourth Universalist Church in February 2001, Cantarella discusses the damaging products of racial stereotyping. Targeting the assumption that blacks lack ambition and have no aspirations, Cantarella describes how these negative images engender conditions that ultimately perpetuate the stereotype and adversely affect black socioeconomic progress. To move beyond racism, Cantarella suggests that society must recognize and affirm the worth and total uniqueness of every individual.

I n 1969 when my father, Whitney Young, wrote the book "Beyond Racism" Blacks in America had cause for optimism. We had seen passed some of the most historic civil rights legislation since the 14th Amendment nearly a hundred years earlier. Civil rights acts guaranteed voting rights, nondiscrimination in housing, public accommodations and employment. Black was beautiful. Our leaders, including my father, graced the covers of *Time* and *Newsweek*. Even our urban rage, destructive though it was, reflected a self-affirming anger. We were mad as hell and not going to take it anymore. No more shuffling obsequies. Through an agenda that became known as "Affirmative Action," there was an institutional effort to redress the impact of past race-based discrimination by taking affirmative steps to include Blacks and others in hiring, purchasing goods and education. We were poised, damn it all, to get "Beyond Racism."

And as most Black folks lived at the margins of American life, the reality was we had to get beyond racism if we were to have any hope at all. In Richard Wright's tremendous novel *Native Son*, the protagonist Bigger Thomas living in a White household sees all that he has not had—the house, the clothes, the fun. By the 1960's, the media had made apparent to all Blacks the difference between their quality of life and that of the Cleaver's or Dick Van Dyke's.

In 1967, the median income for Whites was $8,300 and for Blacks only $4,900—59% of White income and less than half what the government said was needed to live in the urban areas where Blacks were dominant.

While we made up 10% of the population, we were 36% of the impoverished. When he wrote in 1969, the unemployment rate was, like today, 4%, but for urban Blacks it was 20%. And Blacks were paid 36–42% less for the same jobs as Whites. This remained true even with a college education.

And so now here we are 30 years after my father's death. Where do we stand according to the National Urban League's State of Black America 2000? While our unemployment rate has gone down for Black Americans, it is still twice as high as White Americans regardless of the level of educational achievement. We are still twice as likely to live in poverty. Yet there has been progress. Not only are more of us attending colleges and professional schools, thanks to affirmative efforts, but as William Bowen and Derek Bok have pointed out in their ground-breaking book, *The Shape of the River*, the impact of that effort has been significant. They document a real premium in both the wages and the levels of satisfaction of those Black students who have been enabled to attend highly selective colleges. The wage gap is less, the civic participation rate higher.

And so progress has been made. And yet we are clearly not "Beyond Racism." A Black man can even now be dragged behind a truck to his death, stopped in New Jersey while driving because he's Black, or have a greater chance of being on death row than in college. While talking to my son, Mark, recently who just bought a home in a White suburb of Boston, he reflected that while shoveling snow from the driveway, he wondered if anyone realized that he was the homeowner and not the handyman. Growing up in an affluent section of NYC he could not get cabs or was followed when visiting his dad in the executive offices at Bloomingdales. Like him, I know that unless I am wearing a suit, I am likely to be taken for a maid in our apartment building. I have heard students over and over, both at NYU and at Princeton, describe the annoyance of being expected to "represent" the race in the classroom where they may be the sole brown face. While biracial marriages increase, the children they produce often find that they must deal with the fact that some part of their identity is less acceptable than the other part. What kind of sense does that make?

Racial Stereotyping

These examples are all the product of racial stereotyping. Unlike White folks, Blacks are somehow expected to be a monolithic, homogeneous people whose characteristics are skewed to the negative. By what reason are we expected to represent such unity when, thanks to miscegenation, forced or voluntary, we share the blood of the French (as in Creole), Scots, British, and every other type who owned slaves—as well as Native Americans and Hispanics. The range of skin colors in the Black population is as rich and nuanced as any palette on earth. And equally rich and nuanced is our range of experiences. In the 19th century you could find us as cooks and cowboys, idlers and intellectuals, poets and plowmen, soldiers and seamstresses, educators and entrepreneurs. And time has only widened the possibilities. We can be computer makers and cabinet members, deans and dentists, attorneys and astronauts. Given the dazzling array of the spectrum of identities represented by Black folks, stereotypes do not sit well with us. I believe that stereotyping is especially grating in America given our national mythology.

Americans believe strongly in individualism and individual freedom. That is the underpinning of the Bill of Rights. Our heroes of fictional fame are all quirky, rugged individualists from James Fennimore Cooper's *Leatherstocking* to every character ever played by Bogart or Tracy or Wayne. While we have been characterized as a nation of sheep and are the home of the mass market, our philosophical origins tilt to the factions of Madison's *Federalist 10,* Emerson's *Self-Reliance* and Ayn Rand's *Atlas Shrugged*. While we need community, we still revel in our individuality. Blacks, immersed in this culture from its very beginnings, are no different. Are John Shaft and Sam Spade very different anti-heroes? Over the past ten years, we have seen more mass marketing give way to niche marketing as technology has made targeting and personalization more possible. If the majority of Americans do not want to be lumped together, Blacks do not either. Stereotyping creates dissonance and discomfort.

One of the most damaging of stereotypes is the one that assumes that Blacks lack ambition and have no aspirations. Again the notion of socio-economic mobility in America was documented as far back as Tocqueville's writings in the 1830's. The brilliant contemporary chronicler of American life, Studs Terkel, studied aspiration in his book *American Dreams: Lost and Found*. What is clear is that in every one of his hundreds of interviews, everyone has a dream, each dream is unique, and the poignancy comes through in the presence or absence of hope. Journalist and NYU professor, David Dent, engaged in a singular exploration exclusively among Black folks. And there resonated again the dreams of "moving on up," "getting a piece of the pie," to lift from the old Jefferson's TV show's theme song. In America, the urge to move up (in status) has become connected to the need for wealth or at the very least celebrity. The tragedy of *Death of a Salesman* was Willie Loman's spiraling down in prestige as his earning power diminished.

Blacks have watched as wave after wave of immigrants has entered America in search of the ability to be self-sufficient, personally free and upwardly mobile. And wave after wave of immigrants—the Irish, the Italians, Jews and now Asians have achieved these goals. They have moved on from the ghettos of the Lower East Side and moved up to the Upper East Side (or here to the even *more* chichi West Side!) And a great many Black folks have also. Yet in the many minds who stereotype us we have never left Harlem. My son can't get a cab because the driver assumes that he lives in Harlem. When I leave my apartment I must be going home to Harlem. Yet let me list for you the Black millionaires that I know: Vernon Jordan, partner at Lazard Freires, Dick Parsons, COO of Time Warner, Ed Lewis, Publisher of *Essence,* and Earl Graves, Publisher of *Black Enterprise.* Then there is Ken Chenault, new CEO of American Express, or Frederick Raines of Fortune 500 Fannie Mae Corp., or Thomas Jones of Citibank.

My childhood in Atlanta in the 1950's was spent in a segregated environment where we could not swim in public pools or play on public tennis courts. So my friends' parents built their own pools and tennis courts. There has been wealth and status and persons of fine educational pedigree throughout our history here. But those are not the dominant median images. Thank God for Bill Cosby. The Huxtable family was more familiar to me than any I have seen on FOX TV which perpetrates cultural myths of ignorance and buffoonery as the Black status quo.

Once these negative images begin to dominate in the minds of employers and teachers and bureaucrats, how is it possible for Blacks to be viewed as unique individuals filled with aspirations and desires? Our true selves are as unseen as Ellison's characterization of the *Invisible Man.* My taste in music runs to romantic ballads and not rap. I can enjoy equally Gordon Parks or Picasso, Brague or Beardon, ribs or risotto. But going through your minds is the thought "but you are an exception." Let me describe a few students I have come to know over the past twelve years, Black students of different backgrounds. There is the chemistry student pursuing his doctorate at Penn, who is fluent in Chinese, and the comparative literature major with masters degrees from Columbia and Oxford who is now an executive at Morgan Stanley. Her sister is a doctor, her mother was a domestic and a caterer. There was the young social worker who loves professional wrestling, the history major who aspires to sports management, the engineer from Ohio who was a Princeton Rhodes finalist, the engineer now at Wharton who filed several patents at Lockheed before he was 25. There was the student from Nashville who won a grant to study the acoustics of St Marks in Venice and went on to become a computer consultant at Anderson. I can go on and on. They are each uniquely gifted, hard-workers and have their own aspirations. What is painful to observe, however, is the extra burden they carry.

The Burden of Being Black

Let me outline a couple of scenarios that may demonstrate what I mean by burdens. A student, whom we will call Tisha, has gone to a good public school in Queens. She has done exceedingly well and been a leader in a variety of organizations. She is encouraged by her teachers to apply to college—to good colleges. Her parents have worked hard to make a comfortable living. Tisha is the oldest and so will be the first in the family to attend college. It is their dream that she will become a doctor and have wealth, prestige and stability. She had done well in her high school biology and chemistry classes, she was kind. They thought she would be a fine doctor. When Tisha filled in her college applications, where it asked possible majors she wrote "biology," and under career goals, she wrote "medicine." Her family proudly told everyone at church that Tisha was going to college to become a doctor. She had become, for her community, the embodiment of the American dream. Once at college many things happened. She took the math placement test and was placed in an entry-level class as her high school had not offered calculus. However, since she had not had calculus she could not take, as a freshman, the chemistry classes needed for pre-med students. Those would have to wait. So she wisely took other courses which were required. She discovered that she loved her anthropology class. While she struggled with math and a biology class much harder than high school, she was getting A's in anthropology and literature. As educators, we hope students will have these experiences where they sort out their strengths, weaknesses and interests. However, Tisha began to panic. Her family and community wanted, needed, her to be a doctor and she was not doing well in math and science. When her parents came for parents' weekend she said that all was well. She could not disappoint them. She was becoming depressed by her sense of failure. Her White roommate, whose parents and even grandparents were college educated, did not understand. So Tisha kept her sadness to herself. Anyway, she did not want to look dumb. People might think she had only gotten in because she was Black and not because she was qualified. In fact, she was beginning to wonder herself with the low math and science grades, if she had indeed been an "affirmative action" selection. So she kept her doubts and fears to herself. She stopped going to meals and gradually came down with the flu. As a result of being ill, her grades in the classes she loved began to suffer. Despite flyers and announcements about support groups, tutors, and counselors, she was afraid to reveal her insecurities because she did not want others to think that she was dumb because she was Black. In her sophomore year she happened to take another anthropology class from a young African American professor. In the professor she saw something she wanted to be. This was a woman, with a doctorate, who looked like her—even had tiny braids. Tisha began to open up with this professor and revealed that ever since she had tutored in high school she had wanted to teach. Anthropology had captured her imagination. She wanted to major in it—but how to tell her parents, her community, that she would not be a doctor. She would be a disappointment. Her professor suggested that the Dean speak to Tisha's parents. By her junior year Tisha had begun again to be involved in campus groups. Once she dropped the pre-med classes, her grades took off as she reveled in this field she had never heard of. This is not at all an uncommon scenario. With the weight of the world on their shoulders, Black students struggle through and persist in challenging courses of study that White kids would drop without a care. Tisha found a Black mentor in her department. However, with only 1200 Black Ph.D.'s graduated annually, those role models and mentors are scarce. Depression, isolation, anger and frustration are the emotions which accompany far too many Tishas on their paths.

But what of the affluent, the middle-class Black youth? Consider a young man named Malcolm. His parents were both attorneys who had met at Yale Law School. They lived in Scarsdale. Malcolm had gone to a superb public school where most of his friends were White. Most of his parents' friends, associates, and neighbors were White. That was the world that he knew. He played tennis and lacrosse. He wore Ralph Lauren and John Weitz ties. He thought he might go to law school or business school. When he got to college his roommate's mother asked what his SAT scores had been, as if to challenge his ability and his right to be there, as if he were somehow not as good as her son who, being White, had gotten in "legitimately." He was angry but said nothing. In classes he found himself expected to comment on issues of inner city Blacks though he had grown up in an upscale suburb. He became angrier. He played lacrosse and, since not many Black students did, most of his alliances were with White students. He began to be criticized by other Black students for not hanging out with them. That made him angry. As these angers, all internalized, built up he began to drink more making it harder to get up in the morning and to make early classes. His grades began to slide. Fortunately an upperclassman spotted what was happening and urged him to talk, and not to internalize his angers, but to give them constructive voice. Ultimately, and with the help of his parents who had themselves lived this experience, he came to understand that the problem was not with him, but with others who were limited in their visions of what he could be.

Pressure to Achieve

For both of these students there was pressure to achieve. It is virtually an axiom of the "American Dream" that each generation will do better than the one before. However, because these students were being perceived as less than others, inherently less than others, their sense of pressure to achieve was more powerful, painful and poignant. To ask for help, to complain of ill treatment was in their minds to affirm what seemed to be thought of them. However, the impact was to create a self-fulfilling prophecy. Both students began acting out in depression, in self-doubt and in anger. They turned on themselves making the victimized the victim. Recent studies show a performance gap between Black and White students in college. We believe that the gap can be attributed directly to the two scenarios I have described. In addition there is evidence that financial pressures, especially the weight of student loans that must be borne by the majority of Black students of the lower middle class (kept there by ongoing wage discrimination) contribute significantly to the attrition of Black students. They often carry more hours of work at school and cannot afford enriching summer experiences. I am proud to say that my institution, Princeton, has just taken the lead in eliminating student loans to further increase our socioeconomic and ethnic diversity.

And so racial stereotyping itself engenders conditions which perpetrate the situations that perpetuate the stereotypes. When people who are set up to fail do so, they are then called failures, and when they don't, they must be exceptional. But the reality is that most Blacks *are* exceptional by that standard. Though set up to fail, most don't. The media, however, most represents the extremes of the spectrum. We must be Cosby or crooks. The vast majority of upwardly striving, hard-working, honest, good Black folks are not newsworthy. And so as long as the rich array of who we are, in all our colors and experiences, dreams and talents, is not recognized, then we will not get beyond racism. The individuality that is so much at the heart of the American ethos must be accorded to Blacks as well. You, each of us, must challenge away first impressions and seek to know us as individuals. We must engage in common cause and come to some degree of mutual respect. And I do mean mutual respect because we have learned through your distrust of our abilities, to distrust your sincerity. Let your actions prove us wrong. Let a first action be to let the media know that they must seek to represent Blacks in breadth. Study yourselves the privileges of Whiteness. Don't take them for granted. They are true. Getting beyond racism means conscious affirmation of the worth and total uniqueness of each individual. It is a position consistent with our claim for the sanctity of human life. We cannot claim certain principles and then apply them selectively. Life, liberty and the pursuit of happiness for me and mine, not you and yours. Liberty and justice for me but not for you. In all our wars, Blacks have fought to preserve those principles for all of us, only to have them consistently denied to many if not most of us. Operating by stereotype we function in a state of imperfect knowledge. The only person we can stand in judgement of, or know well, is ourselves. Operating from a willingness to learn from and value everyone we encounter, we can grow beyond racism.

Racial Equality in America

Franklin Raines

Franklin Raines is chairman and CEO of Fannie Mae, the largest nonbank financial services company in the world. A graduate of Harvard Law School, Raines's distinguished career includes two years in President Bill Clinton's cabinet as director of the Office of Management and Budget (OMB).

In the following speech delivered at Howard University's Charter Day convocation in March 2002, Raines offers compelling evidence that black Americans have not achieved full equality in American society. Using historical anecdotes, Raines explains how the United States established one of the world's strongest systems of property rights and protections, yet prevented blacks—intentionally according to Raines—from owning assets that could generate capital. Raines concludes that this denial of capital has had devastating consequences in the black community—most notably maintaining the wealth gap between blacks and whites and hindering black socioeconomic mobility.

We are all here today because we stand on the shoulders of giants. And the giants have had great expectations. Dr. [Martin Luther] King once said, "I refuse to accept the idea that an individual is mere flotsam and jetsam in the river of life unable to influence the unfolding events which surround him."

The good fortune that brought us to this room gives us a

special ability—and a special responsibility—to influence events unfolding around us.

What Are the Events That Demand Our Influence?

We gather at an auspicious time for our nation. After a decade of peace, prosperity, and progress, we are met by an unexpected peril. Not just the peril of terrorism and war. We face a peril of self-delusion as well.

A few weeks ago, a newspaper here in Washington carried a four-part series titled, "Black Money." It said that life for African Americans has never been better, suggesting that the quest for racial equality in America was complete.

In fact, that is what most Americans believe. In a major national poll last year, a majority said when it comes to jobs, income, health care, and education, black Americans are doing just as well as whites.

Well, we looked at the facts. And then we asked, "What would life be like if the majority of Americans were right? What if the racial gaps were closed? What would we gain?" So we did the math.

If America had racial equality in education and jobs, African Americans would have two million more high school degrees . . . two million more college degrees . . . nearly two million more professional and managerial jobs . . . and nearly $200 billion more income.

If America had racial equality in housing, three million more African Americans would own their homes.

And if America had racial equality in wealth, African Americans would have $760 billion more in home equity value. Two hundred billion dollars more in the stock market. One hundred twenty billion dollars more in their retirement funds. And $80 billion more in the bank. That alone would total over $1 trillion more in wealth.

These gaps demonstrate that the long journey of black Americans from an enslaved people to full participants in our society—a journey that began 137 years ago—is far from complete.

We have come a long way. We have won the equal right

to education, to employment, to housing, and to success. And yet the racial gaps persist. Why is that? How can we close the gaps?

"The Mystery of Capital"

Perhaps we can find an answer in a recent book by Hernando de Soto, the founder and president of the Institute for Liberty and Democracy in Peru. The book is called, *The Mystery of Capital*. And in it, de Soto has set forth a provocative theory.

He points out that no matter where you go in the world, from the most teeming cities to the remotest villages, people of the most modest means are working hard, producing, trading and selling goods, operating cottage industries, even building and improving homes for their families.

Maybe they own assets—tools, machines, equipment, buildings, livestock. And perhaps they are earning a daily living by harnessing those assets. But here's the problem. No matter how hard they work, they are not able to raise capital against those assets to create wealth. Their assets don't have life beyond their immediate use. These assets, he says, contain "dead capital."

But in America, he points out, assets have two lives. You can live off them. And you can leverage capital from them, unleashing wealth.

Let me illustrate this concept.

When you own a home in America, this asset has daily value as shelter. But it also has value as an investment.

Take these new town homes here in LeDroit Park. Three years ago, the average sale price was about $157,000. Since then, property values in Washington have appreciated a great deal. Today, those homes are worth an average of $224,000. By appreciating in value, these assets generated about $67,000 in capital gains.

In fact, last year homeowners in America withdrew about $80 billion in equity wealth out of their homes. And with that wealth, they paid down credit cards and pumped about $50 billion back into the economy, which provided a bigger economic stimulus than the tax rebate.

Assets in the United States produce capital so well, de

Soto explains, because over the past two centuries, we have developed one of the most sophisticated systems in the world for recording and protecting the ownership of assets. This system evolved from the way that pioneers claimed and settled the frontier, which created a strong tradition of—and quest for—individual property rights in America.

Today, we have titles on our homes and cars. Land records. Property registers. Patents. Copyrights. Contracts. And because you can prove ownership, you can more easily buy and sell your assets, insure them against loss, borrow against them, and protect them in court. And you can more easily pass your assets on to your children.

As de Soto points out, much of the developing world does not have this airtight system of asset protection. Or the system does not recognize everyone's assets, or guarantee everyone's legal rights to protect them.

As a result, he says, "at least 80 percent of the population in these countries cannot inject life into their assets and make them generate capital because the law keeps them out of the formal property system."

As you read de Soto's book, it dawns on you: He's talking about 80 percent of the population in developing countries. But what he is saying also applies to 12 percent of the population in our country, the formerly enslaved. As our country was establishing one of the world's strongest systems of property rights and protections, the formerly enslaved were denied the right to inject life into their assets and make them generate capital.

This denial of black capital has been anything but unintentional. The legacy of slavery, segregation and discrimination—de facto and de jure—systematically kept the formerly enslaved out of the formal property system.

Let me explore this history a little bit.

For their first 250 years in America, the majority of African Americans not only had no property rights—they were property.

Emancipation was supposed to change all of that. The 14th Amendment said the formerly enslaved could not be deprived of life, liberty, or property. And slaves who fought in the Civil War were promised they would receive "40 acres of land and an army mule to work the land."

You've probably heard this phrase before, "40 acres and a mule." And some of you may know that the story behind it has special meaning for this university.

Apparently, toward the end of the Civil War, General Sherman issued Special Field Order Number 15, which said, and I quote:

The islands of Charleston south, the abandoned rice fields along the rivers for 30 miles back from the sea, and the country bordering the St. John's River, Florida, are reserved and set apart for the settlement of the Negroes now made free by the acts of war and the proclamation of the President of the United States.

Sherman ordered this abandoned and forfeited land to be distributed in 40-acre parcels to every freed slave that his troops encountered. And each was to be furnished a title of possession. By June of 1865, about 40,000 former slaves had settled on the land.

Incidentally, this land below Charleston includes what are now the resort islands of Hilton Head and Kiawah, and some of the most beautiful and valuable beachfront property on the Eastern Seaboard.

History buffs might also remind us that the 40-acres plan was assigned to the Army Bureau of Refugees, Freedmen, and Abandoned Lands. And this bureau was led by none other than General Oliver Otis Howard—the same General Howard who led this university, and for whom it is named.

But of course, General Howard never got to implement the plan, because President Andrew Johnson caved to political pressure and invalidated Sherman's order in favor of the previous white landowners. So instead of owning the property, former slaves who wanted to stay there had to work for the former slaveholders.

This was just the beginning of the century-long process that denied former slaves access to property and its power to create wealth.

The black codes and Jim Crow laws made a mockery of the 14th Amendment's protection of property rights for the freed slaves. Many states began to limit the types of property blacks could own. In Texas, the homestead law explicitly prohibited the distribution of public land to blacks.

And even when former slaves were allowed to settle open land or purchase property, it wasn't easy to keep it.

For example, at the Jim Crow oral history project at the Studio Museum in Harlem, there's a story about a freedman who was encouraged by his white employer to purchase a coveted piece of real estate. The employer even helped negotiate a federal loan. But the employer's sons disagreed, and somehow, the freedman's house was burned to the ground, killing his younger brother and sister.

All over the South, terrorists in white robes systematically drove black families from their land and businesses. And it is a bitter irony that for much of the 20th century, this country's system of property rights was used to deny black Americans their property rights.

For example, you may be familiar with Levittown on Long Island, the first major planned suburb in America. It was developed in 1947 to help house the GI's returning from World War II and their families. That is, except for the 1.2 million black Americans who served in the war, because each Levittown home came with a restrictive covenant that said, "The tenant agrees not to permit the premises to be used or occupied by any person other than members of the Caucasian race."

Even here in Washington, DC, African Americans had trouble closing the purchase of a home because some of the deeds included language that said, "It is covenanted and agreed that the above described property and no part thereof, shall ever be sold, transferred, leased, rented to, nor occupied by any Negro or person of African blood."

Racial covenants were even written into the FHA underwriting manual, and it wasn't until 1948 that the Supreme Court outlawed racial covenants.

Property ownership among African Americans receded throughout the 20th century. In 1920, blacks owned about 15 million acres of land. Today, they hold only 1.1 million acres. This shocking loss of property, one observer said, represents "a massive wealth transfer out of the black community."

How did this happen? According to an investigation by

the Associated Press, many black families have been driven from or swindled out of their property. Many lost their farmland, business property and even homes because they did not have wills. Or family land was partitioned, auctioned and sold out from under them.

But even those African Americans who could obtain and protect their property could not always get full use of it because they could not capitalize it to build wealth.

The Denial of Capital

This brings us back to our Peruvian economist, Hernando de Soto, and his concept that assets have a second life because they generate capital.

That is what made the promise of "40 acres and a mule" so attractive. With this property, the freedmen not only could raise crops to support their families; they could raise capital to support their futures.

But here again, African Americans have been denied the ability to raise capital against their property.

In fact, just three years ago, black farmers won a class-action suit against the U.S. Department of Agriculture for years of discrimination in farm lending practices, and each farmer won damages of $50,000.

A similar problem has persisted in home lending.

You are all familiar with the term "redlining." For years, banks refused to make loans in certain neighborhoods. They literally drew a red line on a map around certain areas, and if you lived inside the red line you were automatically rejected.

Redlining was outlawed in 1968. But in 1992, the Federal Reserve Bank of Boston published a landmark study that showed why black mortgage applicants were rejected more often than white applicants were. Essentially, if two loan applications needed a little extra work, the white family would get help, while the black family would be rejected.

Today, most mortgage applications are processed by automated underwriting systems, which are colorblind because the borrower's race is not even entered into the computer. This technology has helped to lift African American mortgage approvals and homeownership.

But a different kind of redlining goes on today.

Black Americans are much more likely than whites to fall into the subprime mortgage market. About 22 percent of the subprime market are African American borrowers.

The problem is that subprime loans have the highest interest rates in the entire market. Subprime loans can cost a borrower up to $200,000 more in interest costs than a Fannie Mae loan. And many subprime borrowers actually could qualify for lower-cost loans, but they're being steered or seduced into the high-cost loan.

Worse than that, inner city neighborhoods are prime targets for predatory lenders, who charge hidden and abusive rates, fees, and rules. And when the borrower gets behind, the predatory lender can seize and sell their homes.

When black Americans who can afford the least are paying the most for housing capital, it is not only a denial of consumer rights. It is a denial of capital rights. And when African Americans cannot obtain capital, or must pay abusive rates for it, it is impossible to leverage their assets to generate wealth.

The wealth gap, in fact, has remained about the same for the last 20 years. We have seen no progress at all. And this lack of wealth in black America helps to explain why the gaps persist in education, jobs, and property ownership.

Without wealth, it's hard to send your kids to college. Without college, it's hard to get a good job. Without a good job, it's hard to earn a good income. Without a good income, it's hard to obtain property. And without property and the capital to leverage it, it's hard to create wealth to send your kids to college. And the chain of denial continues. . . .

Studies tell us that homeownership leads to stronger families and safer, more close-knit communities with better schools and services. Children go farther and do better in school. And so homeownership can help to close the gaps in education, and thus, jobs and income.

But homeownership is absolutely critical to closing the wealth gap. Owning a home is the working man and woman's capital engine, the democratization of capital. More Americans earn more wealth owning a home than they do investing in the stock market. Owning a home is the most important investment—and the only leveraged investment—available to most Americans. It is a powerful way to transmit wealth from generation to generation.

For African Americans—the formerly enslaved—home-ownership has the power to help to mend the broken promise of "40 acres and a mule."

Appendix of Biographies

Marcia Cantarella

Marcia Cantarella, born October 31, 1946, is the daughter of Whitney Young Jr., the highly regarded civil rights leader who directed the Urban League during the peak of the civil rights movement during the 1960s. Cantarella is an assistant dean at Princeton University, where she has held many academic positions and lectures on a variety of topics. Her areas of specialty include business management and administration, women's entrepreneurship, and American studies.

Throughout her career, Cantarella has dedicated herself to the empowerment of women. As the former executive director of the National Coalition for Women's Enterprise, for example, Cantarella promoted women's rights in the workplace and training for self-employment. Among her many business affiliations are the Association of Black Foundation Executives and Women and Foundations Group.

Currently, Cantarella uses her business expertise to support the Trickle Up program, an international nonprofit organization that promotes the worldwide expansion of small businesses to bolster economic growth and uplift impoverished people.

Stokely Carmichael

Born in 1941 in Trinidad, British West Indies, Stokely Carmichael moved to New York City with his family when he was eleven. An excellent student in high school, Carmichael was offered scholarships to several prestigious—but predominantly white—universities. He rejected those offers and instead enrolled at Howard University, where he majored in philosophy. During his freshman year, Carmichael participated in Freedom Rides—interracial bus trips that protested segregation on public transportation—that were sponsored by the Congress of Racial Equality. As a result of those rides, he was arrested and jailed frequently, once serving a forty-nine-day sentence.

Carmichael graduated in 1964 and soon after joined the Student Nonviolent Coordinating Committee (SNCC), participating in a number of demonstrations and voter registration drives throughout the South. Intelligent and charismatic, Carmichael was appointed chairman of SNCC in 1966. By that time, however, Carmichael had grown disillusioned with the organization's philosophy of nonviolence. With his rallying cry of "black power," Carmichael led SNCC to shift its focus from integration and nonviolence to black nationalism at any cost.

Carmichael left SNCC in 1967 to become prime minister of the more militant Black Panthers. Little more than a year later, Carmichael—who had changed his name to Kwame Ture to reflect his African roots—moved to Africa and became affiliated with the All-African People's Revolutionary Party, a Marxist organization that sought to unify the nations of Africa. Although he lived the rest of his life in Africa, he returned to the United States often to bolster Pan-African causes. He died in 1998.

Morris Dees

The son of a farmer, Morris Dees was born in 1936 in rural Alabama. Raised in the South, Dees—although from a fairly well-to-do family himself—witnessed the harmful effects of racism and discrimination. He attended the University of Alabama, graduating from the School of Law in 1960. Soon after, he opened a law office in Montgomery. At the same time, he continued to operate a successful mail order and book publishing company that he had launched while an undergraduate student.

In the late 1960s, Dees took the fight for minority rights into the courtroom. Although he angered many in the white community—among his many controversial cases, he fought to empower blacks and end segregation, for example—he gained popularity throughout the predominantly black South.

As he continued his advocacy for blacks, the poor, and other disfranchised minorities, Dees and his law partner founded the Southern Poverty Law Center, a nonprofit legal center that specializes in civil rights violations and racially motivated crimes. As chief trial counsel for the center, Dees has won a number of landmark cases. In one high-profile trial, for example, Dees won a $12.5 million judgment against Tom Metzger and the White Aryan Resistance for their role in the death of a black student in Oregon. In conjunction with his legal activities, Dees promotes "Teaching Tolerance," the center's highly regarded educational program designed to combat hatred and discrimination.

Frederick Douglass

The son of a slave woman and an unknown white man, Frederick Douglass was born Frederick Augustus Washington Bailey in 1818 on a Maryland farm. At the age of six, Bailey was put to work in the fields, where the impressionable young boy learned firsthand the unbearably harsh conditions slaves were forced to endure, suffering not only from the woefully inadequate food, clothing, and shelter but also the frequent and brutal beatings. Two years later, Bailey was sent to live in Baltimore to work as a house slave for a shipbuilder. Under the tutelage of his master's wife, Bailey learned to read. He also learned that there were people called abolitionists who fought to end slavery. Douglass later commented on his stay in Baltimore that it "laid the foundation and opened the gateway to all my subsequent prosperity."

After eight years in Baltimore, Bailey was sent to work for a notoriously cruel slave master. Starved, beaten, and weakened, a resolute Bailey began to plot his own emancipation. By 1838, Bailey was back in Baltimore, where he worked in a shipyard. While not working, Bailey spent time with a group of educated black teachers from the Sabbath School, where he not only honed his writing and speaking skills but also enjoyed the intellectually stimulating environment. Still longing for freedom, however, Bailey—disguised as a sailor and carrying fake documents—boarded a train bound for New York.

Bailey arrived safely in the North and, hoping to elude detection, changed his name to Douglass. In Massachusetts, Douglass became active in the abolitionist movement and joined the American Anti-Slavery Society led by William Lloyd Garrison. Shortly thereafter, Douglass addressed the society for the first time. One correspondent found Douglass's speech so compelling that "flinty hearts were pierced, and cold ones melted by his eloquence." Garrison, too, recognized Douglass's skills as a public speaker and hired the former slave to lecture Northern audiences on behalf of the Massachusetts Anti-Slavery Society—effectively launching Douglass's career in the public spotlight.

Douglass—now famous but still an escaped slave—became fearful of reprisals and fled to Great Britain to avoid possible reenslavement. There, Douglass earned enough money to buy his own freedom. When he returned to America in 1847, Douglass settled in Rochester, New York, where he published the *North Star,* an abolitionist newspaper that also supported women's rights. At the same time, Douglass helped direct the Underground Railroad, the network that harbored and assisted runaway slaves. With the Emancipation Proclamation, Douglass focused his efforts on the black suffrage movement. He continued to work tirelessly to better the lives of blacks until his death in 1895.

W.E.B. Du Bois

William Edward Burghardt Du Bois was born in Massachusetts in 1868—three years after the end of the Civil War. Abandoned by his father, Du Bois was raised by his mother, Mary. Although relatively poor—Mary's income as a household servant was meager—the young Du Bois proved himself to be not only academically gifted but also industrious and highly motivated to succeed. Upon graduation from high school, Du Bois attended Fisk University in Nashville, Tennessee. During school breaks, Du Bois worked at a rural school in eastern Tennessee, where he witnessed firsthand the miserable conditions endured by impoverished Southern blacks. Deeply moved by their plight, Du Bois dedicated his life to uplifting people of all races.

After graduating as valedictorian from Fisk University, Du Bois enrolled at Harvard. He would become the first African American to earn a Ph.D. from that prestigious institution. A consummate scholar, Du Bois embarked on what would become a distinguished career in education, teaching Latin and Greek at Wilberforce University in Ohio and later at the University of Pennsylvania. He also served as professor of economics and history at Atlanta University.

By 1897 Du Bois was conducting research that focused on the subject of race and the problems of black society in America. Over the course of his groundbreaking work, Du Bois came to conclude that only agitation and social protest could combat institutionalized racism. At the turn of the century, Du Bois devoted himself to another cause: Pan-Africanism, the movement to free Africa from foreign control and establish a free black nation.

In 1909 Du Bois helped found the National Association for the Advancement of Colored People (NAACP), serving as the group's director of publications and editor of its *Crisis* magazine until 1934. Between 1944 and 1948, Du Bois headed the NAACP's special research department. Alongside these endeavors, the indefatigable Du Bois continued to speak out against racism and publish numerous books and articles, including *The Souls of Black Folk* (1903), *The Gift of Black Folk* (1924), and *Color and Democracy* (1945), among many others. In 1961 Du Bois immigrated to Africa and became editor-in-chief of the *Encyclopedia Africana*. He died in Ghana in 1953 at the age of ninety-five.

James Farmer

James Farmer was born in 1920 in Marshall, Texas. He was raised in a home that viewed education as a tool to remedy society's ills.

His father, J. Leonard Farmer, was a religious scholar and teacher—and one of the few African Americans in Texas to hold a Ph.D. As a child, Farmer excelled academically, entering Wiley College at the age of fourteen. Upon graduation, Farmer entered Howard University's School of Theology. Although he elected not to enter the ministry—he was opposed to segregation within the church—Farmer's religious faith remained an important facet of both his private and public life.

Farmer joined the struggle for civil rights in 1941 when he went to work for the Fellowship of Reconciliation, a pacifist organization that sought to alleviate poverty and violence. A year later, Farmer and several associates formed the Congress of Racial Equality (CORE), the first American civil rights organization to implement nonviolent tactics in the fight for racial equality.

In 1961 CORE, under the leadership of Farmer, made national headlines when it organized the first Freedom Ride, in which volunteers traveled on buses throughout the South in an effort to desegregate interstate buses and bus terminals. Freedom Riders were met with fierce, sometimes violent, resistance. In one particularly perilous incident, a Freedom Rider bus was burned to the ground, leaving its occupants barely time to escape the inferno.

Although Farmer left CORE in 1966, he continued to speak out against civil rights abuses. He taught for a time at Lincoln University in Pennsylvania, and in 1969 he served President Richard Nixon as assistant director of Health, Education, and Welfare. Farmer died in 1999, a year after President Bill Clinton awarded the civil rights activist the Medal of Freedom, America's highest civilian honor.

Fannie Lou Hamer

Fannie Lou Hamer was an unlikely heroine of the civil rights movement. The daughter of sharecroppers, Hamer spent much of her life in poverty in the rural South. Yet through extraordinary determination and a passionate desire to improve the lives of blacks, Hamer rose from her humble beginnings to become an eloquent spokesperson and crusader in the struggle for black rights.

Born in Mississippi in 1918, Hamer was the twentieth child of Jim and Lou Ella Townsend. Like her siblings, Hamer began to work in the cotton fields when she was six years old. She attended school for a brief period but was forced to drop out so that she could help support her family in the fields. Although life was hard, Hamer continued her education by reading and studying the Bible with members of the Stranger's Home Baptist Church. Likewise, her mother taught her to maintain pride and respect for herself.

As Hamer continued working as a sharecropper, an event occurred that would change the course of her life: In 1962 Hamer and seventeen other blacks took a bus to the county seat to register to vote. For this simple act, Hamer was arrested, jailed, and fired from the plantation on which she had worked for eighteen years.

Despite her troubles, Hamer attended a conference of the Student Nonviolent Coordinating Committee (SNCC). Soon, she was appointed field secretary of SNCC and began implementing voter registration programs. In 1963 Hamer successfully registered to vote, but she could not pay the expensive poll taxes that were designed to prohibit poor Southern blacks from voting. Several months later, she was arrested and brutally beaten after attending a voter registration workshop.

In 1964 Hamer, representing the Mississippi Freedom Democratic Party, spoke to the Credentials Committee at the 1964 Democratic National Convention. In her televised testimony, Hamer brought into living rooms across America the injustices that blacks were forced to endure. Until her death in 1977, Hamer remained active in the civil rights arena, organizing grassroots initiatives to benefit rural communities and helping to found the National Women's Political Caucus.

Jesse Jackson

Jesse Jackson was born in 1941 in South Carolina. The discrimination Jackson experienced as a youth led to his lifelong passion to fight racial inequality. Driven to overcome the forces that oppressed young blacks, Jackson graduated at the top of his high school class and later graduated from North Carolina Agricultural and Technical State University. After postgraduate work at Chicago Theological Seminary, he was ordained a Baptist minister in 1968.

Jackson became active in the civil rights movement in 1965, when he joined the Southern Christian Leadership Conference, and, within two years, assumed a leadership role in the organization. By that time, Jackson—with a charismatic personality and close personal ties to Martin Luther King Jr.—was a highly visible civil rights leader. With a host of committed followers, he founded two organizations: Operation PUSH (People United to Save Humanity) in 1971 and, in 1984, the National Rainbow Coalition, an organization that promoted the rights of a wide array of minority groups, including Hispanics and gays.

Jackson's political aspirations led to two unsuccessful bids for the U.S. presidency during the 1980s. Since then, Jackson has continued to operate the Rainbow Coalition out of Washington, D.C., where he speaks, writes, and dabbles in foreign affairs. Although at times his career has been touched by personal scandal and controversy, Jackson remains a compelling advocate for oppressed people throughout the world.

Lyndon B. Johnson

Lyndon B. Johnson was born in 1908 near Johnson City, Texas. Although the Johnson family had been prominent in Texas for generations, during Lyndon's childhood the family farm was not producing and the family lived on the verge of bankruptcy. Johnson did not stand out academically at the public grade school, but he went on to Southwest Texas State Teachers College in San Marcos, Texas. He worked with many impoverished rural children when he taught grade school students the year following his graduation.

Johnson embarked on a career in politics in 1931, relocating to Washington, D.C., as an aide to a Texas congressman. He enjoyed the political arena immensely and established a wide network of friends. In 1937 Johnson successfully campaigned for Congress, where he worked closely with President Franklin D. Roosevelt. During World War II, Johnson was commissioned in the naval reserves for a brief time before returning to the nation's capital. In 1950 Johnson became a senator, and by 1954 he had advanced to the post of Senate majority leader.

Buoyed by his successes in Congress, Johnson campaigned for the Democratic presidential nomination in 1960. He lost to John F. Kennedy, but he went on to became Kennedy's vice president. Upon Kennedy's assassination on November 22, 1963, Johnson entered the White House as the thirty-sixth president of the United States.

The new president's domestic program was popular; Johnson launched the "War on Poverty" and also secured passage of the Civil Rights Act of 1964 and the Voting Rights Act a year later. At the same time, however, the nation was becoming increasingly involved in the Vietnam War. As the administration continued to commit resources to that war, however, American opposition to the war grew. As a result, Johnson's popularity plummeted. In 1968 Johnson announced that he would not seek reelection. He died in 1973.

John F. Kennedy

Born in 1917 in Brookline, Massachusetts, John F. Kennedy enjoyed a happy childhood. His large Catholic family—Kennedy was the second of nine children—was not only politically connected but also wealthy, with the means to support a lavish lifestyle.

Despite his privileged upbringing, the young Kennedy worked hard to distinguish himself. He attended private schools before studying at Harvard University, where he graduated with honors in 1940. Shortly thereafter, Kennedy enlisted in the U.S. Navy. With World War II raging in the Pacific, Kennedy volunteered for combat duty in the Solomon Islands. His bravery and devotion to his crew—he was in command of a torpedo boat—earned him high praise at the war's close.

After a brief stint as a newspaper reporter in 1945, Kennedy decided to pursue a political career in Boston. With a campaign slogan of "Kennedy will do more for Massachusetts," he was elected to the U.S. Congress in 1946, ultimately serving three terms in the House of Representatives and, starting in 1952, eight years in the Senate. A popular and charismatic leader, Kennedy announced his candidacy for the U.S. presidency during the late fifties. With a platform based on the civil, economic, and political rights of man, Kennedy narrowly won the 1960 presidential race against Richard Nixon. At the age of forty-three, Kennedy was the youngest person—and the first Roman Catholic—to be elected president.

Throughout his presidential career, Kennedy confronted many political challenges, including the Cuban missile crisis, which brought the United States and the former Soviet Union to the brink of nuclear war. Kennedy's domestic program included support for significant civil rights reforms, including the desegregation of public schools.

In November 1963 Kennedy was shot and killed while riding in a motorcade in Dallas, Texas. He died in the arms of his wife, Jackie, who had been riding next to him in the open vehicle.

Martin Luther King Jr.

Few African American leaders had as much impact on the civil rights movement—and the American consciousness—as Martin Luther King Jr. Born in 1929 at his home in Atlanta, Georgia, King attended Ebenezer Baptist Church, where both his father and grandfather—active civil rights leaders themselves—were employed as ministers. Because King grew up surrounded by a loving family in a fairly well-to-do home, he was somewhat sheltered from the sting of racism. He was not completely immune to the harsh effects of discrimination, however, and—even as a youth—King desperately wanted to improve the lives of blacks and viewed the church as an instrument for change.

Intelligent and determined, King entered Morehouse College at the age of fifteen. Inspired by Benjamin Mays, then president of the college, King decided to become a minister so that he could better society. Following graduate studies at Crozer Theological Seminary, King received a doctorate in systematic theology from Boston University in 1955. Feeling a moral obligation to serve his fellow man in the South, King—recently married to Coretta Scott—accepted a position as pastor of the Dexter Avenue Baptist Church in Montgomery, Alabama.

In 1955 a woman named Rosa Parks made history when she defied Montgomery's mandated segregation on buses. King—well known for his persuasive sermons that often centered on racial injustices—was elected president of the Montgomery Improvement Association, an organization formed to spearhead a massive boycott of the city's buses. King gained national acclaim when the U.S. Supreme Court declared Alabama's segregation laws unconstitutional. In 1957 King and other Southern black leaders founded the Southern Christian Leadership Conference to mobilize and create social change through the use of nonviolent techniques. King directed the organization's civil rights activities until his death in 1968. At the same time, he served as copastor with his father at Ebenezer Baptist Church in Atlanta.

In 1963, King launched mass demonstrations in Birmingham, Alabama, where blacks suffered abuses at the hands of white police officials. The resulting clashes between police and protesters generated headlines around the world, as did the subsequent March on Washington, a demonstration that attracted 250,000 protesters to the nation's capital in 1963. There, King delivered his famous "I Have a Dream" speech.

In the years following the March on Washington, King's renown grew as he continued to speak, write, and organize protests, including the famous 1965 Selma-to-Montgomery march. King was arrested numerous times for these activities, but he remained undaunted in his quest to end discrimination and secure equal rights for all Americans. In 1968 King was shot and mortally wounded in Memphis, Tennessee.

John Lewis

John Lewis was born into a family of sharecroppers in 1940, outside of Troy, Alabama. Impoverished and forced to attend a segregated public school, Lewis developed an early interest in civil rights issues. Determined and hardworking, Lewis graduated from the American Baptist Theological Seminary in Nashville, Tennessee, and went on to receive a bachelor's degree in religion and philosophy from Fisk University. As a seminary student, Lewis joined the Student Nonviolent Coordinating Committee (SNCC), an organization that advocated peaceful protest to promote social equality. In 1961 Lewis became a Freedom Rider, traveling alongside whites through the Deep South to protest segregation on buses and in interstate bus terminals.

By 1963 Lewis—only twenty-three years old—was widely respected for his civil rights activism, and he was elected chairperson of SNCC. The same year, Lewis helped organize the historic March on Washington. In the company of Martin Luther King Jr. and other well-known individuals, Lewis delivered a keynote address that condemned discrimination and segregation in American society. Two years later, Lewis led five hundred marchers in Selma, Alabama. The historic incident would become known as "Bloody Sunday" after state troopers viciously attacked the peaceful protesters.

Although Lewis left SNCC in 1966, he remained active in the civil rights movement and committed to the philosophy of nonviolence. He continued to promote voter registration programs and was elected by President Jimmy Carter in 1977 to direct ACTION, a federal volunteer agency.

Lewis launched a political career in 1981 when he was elected to serve on the Atlanta City Council. In 1986 Lewis was elected to Congress, representing Georgia's Fifth Congressional District. In 2002 Lewis was serving his eighth term in office.

Malcolm X

Born Malcolm Little in 1925, Malcolm X rose from a life of poverty to profoundly influence black America. Following a series of family calamities—his father was murdered and his mother was placed in a mental institution—Malcolm spent much of his childhood in foster homes and detention centers.

In 1941 Malcolm was sent to live in Boston, where he lost interest in school and took up a life of petty crime. While in prison for burglary at the age of twenty-one, Malcolm became a follower of Elijah Muhammad, the spiritual leader of the Nation of Islam, a sect that blended Islam and black nationalism. Malcolm adopted his new religion wholeheartedly, adhering to the strict teachings of Muhammad and changing his last name to "X" to signify his lost tribal connections.

After his parole in 1952, Malcolm continued a close association with Elijah Muhammad. Fiery, charismatic, and intelligent, Malcolm was sent on speaking tours to bolster membership in the

Black Muslim movement. Preaching black pride, economic self-reliance, and separation of the races, Malcolm attracted a large following. By the late 1950s, Malcolm had not only greatly expanded the Nation of Islam; he had also emerged as the movement's most important leader.

In 1963 Malcolm learned that Elijah Muhammad was having extramarital affairs, behavior strictly forbidden by the Nation of Islam. Malcolm was openly critical of his mentor, creating tension within the movement. Malcolm broke with the Nation of Islam in 1964 and, after a trip to Mecca, birthplace of the prophet Muhammad, came to embrace a more moderate approach to black nationalism. One year later, Malcolm was assassinated while giving a speech in New York City.

Nelson Mandela

South Africa's first black president was born in 1918 in Transkei, South Africa. His father was a chief of the Tembu, a Xhosa-speaking tribe. In 1939 Mandela enrolled at Fort Hare University, but he was expelled after three years for leading a boycott of the Student Representative Council. He earned a law degree—and ultimately set up South Africa's first black law firm—at the University of South Africa, during which time he lived in Alexandra Township. There, the squalid living conditions and the area's appalling racist policies led Mandela to join the African National Congress (ANC) in 1944. As a member of the ANC, Mandela sought to dismantle the apartheid policies of the National Party, which ruled South Africa.

By 1950, Mandela had assumed presidency of the ANC. As he intensified the league's anti-apartheid campaign, he was tried for treason in 1956 but was finally acquitted in 1961. After the ANC was banned in 1960, Mandela was arrested for organizing a military branch of the organization, the Umkhonto we Sizwe (Spear of the Nation), and in 1962 he was sentenced to five years of hard labor. The following year, Mandela—still serving the five-year sentence—faced even more severe charges; he was accused of sabotage and attempting to overthrow the South African government. By trial's end in 1964, Mandela had been sentenced to life in prison.

During his time in prison, Mandela endured extremely harsh conditions. At the same time, he became a potent symbol of black liberation. He was released from prison in February 1990. The following year, at the first national conference held since the organization was banned four decades earlier, Mandela was elected president of the ANC. He continues to promote democracy and racial equality.

Thurgood Marshall

The son of a dining room steward and a teacher, Thurgood Marshall was born in 1908 in Maryland. He spent his youth in Baltimore, where his teachers at the public school recognized his academic abilities early on. After graduating from Lincoln University, Marshall studied law at Howard University, graduating with honors in 1933.

The same year, Marshall launched a private legal practice in Baltimore. Early in his new career, Marshall—already known to champion minority causes—caught the attention of the National Association for the Advancement of Colored People. Marshall became the organization's legal director in 1940, a post he would hold until 1961. During those years, Marshall's primary goal was to formulate legal strategies to overturn racial segregation in housing, voting, and education. In his most well-known case, Marshall served as chief counsel in the historic *Brown v. Board of Education,* which declared racial segregation in public schools illegal. Overall, with his brilliant legal mind and straightforward manner, Marshall won thirty-two of the thirty-five cases that he argued before the Supreme Court.

In 1961 Marshall entered public service when he was nominated by President John F. Kennedy to the Second Court of Appeals. Four years later, President Lyndon B. Johnson appointed him solicitor general of the United States. Then, on August 30, 1967, Marshall, again nominated by Johnson, became the first African American justice to sit on the Supreme Court of the United States. In his twenty-three-year tenure as a Supreme Court justice, Marshall became known for his unrepentant liberal views and his efforts to uplift the poor and oppressed. He retired from the High Court in 1991 and died of heart failure three years later.

Franklin Raines

Born in 1949 and raised in the Pacific Northwest, Franklin Raines rose from poverty to build a formidable career in politics and business. Determined and academically gifted, Raines obtained a law degree from Harvard University and also attended Oxford University as a Rhodes scholar.

Raines's myriad endeavors include his appointment as associate director for economics and government in the Office of Management and Budget (OMB) in 1977. During the 1980s, Raines was a partner with Lazard Freres & Company, a leading financial advisory firm. In 1996 Raines went to work in President Bill Clinton's cabinet as OMB director. During his two-year tenure, Raines became the first director in a generation to balance the federal budget.

In 1998 Raines stepped down from his cabinet-level post to take over as chairman and chief executive officer–designate of Fannie Mae, the world's largest nonbank financial services company and the nation's largest source of home financing. Through his work with Fannie Mae, Raines remains dedicated to improving and equalizing economic opportunities for all underprivileged Americans.

A. Philip Randolph

The son of a Methodist preacher, Asa Philip Randolph was born in 1889 in Crescent City, Florida. His family moved to Jacksonville in 1891, where the young Randolph graduated at the top of his high school class. In 1911 Randolph moved to New York and took classes at City College, during which time he joined the Socialist Party.

Early in his career, Randolph came to view well-paying jobs and economic opportunity as the most important tools in the fight for racial equality. In 1917 Randolph and a friend, Chandler Owen, established an employment agency that catered to black workers. Politically like-minded, Randolph and Owen founded a magazine, the *Messenger,* a radical publication that called for more black opportunity in the war industry. Also during this time Randolph rallied black opposition to World War I and, in several instances, garnered support for black workers on strike. In 1925 Randolph launched the Brotherhood of Sleeping Car Porters to organize workers of the Pullman Company. Despite many setbacks, Randolph continued his efforts and, in 1937, Pullman finally signed a contract with the black union—an unprecedented event at the time.

With his successes as a labor leader in the 1930s, Randolph became a highly visible spokesperson for black rights. With World War II unfolding, Randolph focused his attention on discrimination in the defense industries. In 1941, when he called a mass gathering of one hundred thousand black workers in Washington, D.C., to demand change, President Franklin D. Roosevelt conceded to Randolph. The march was called off, and Roosevelt signed an executive order banning discrimination in the government and defense industries that received federal funds.

Randolph continued to press for black economic freedom. In 1948, he persuaded President Truman to sign an order that would abolish Jim Crow laws in the armed forces. In 1963, reminiscent of his activities surrounding the proposed march of 1941, Randolph was named director of the March on Washington. Randolph retired from the public eye in 1969. He died ten years later, just one month after his ninetieth birthday.

Bayard Rustin

Bayard Rustin was born in 1912 in West Chester, Pennsylvania. In high school, the young Rustin was a gifted student, athlete, and musician. He attended both Wilberforce University and Cheyney State College before moving to New York and enrolling in the City College of New York in 1937. Although he never received a degree, Rustin would remain in New York for the rest of his life.

At City College, Rustin launched his career as a political activist when he went to work for the Young Communist League, an organization that targeted racial problems as it maintained a strong antiwar stance. A committed pacifist, Rustin spent three years behind bars for refusing to register for the draft during World War II.

After he quit the Young Communist League in 1941, Rustin went to work for A. Philip Randolph, the preeminent black leader who led the Brotherhood of Sleeping Car Porters, a black trade union. At the same time, Rustin worked to improve race relations through his affiliation with A.J. Muste, leader of the Fellowship of Reconciliation.

Rustin worked alongside Martin Luther King Jr. in organizing the bus boycott that would end discrimination in public transportation. Rustin also directed the historic March on Washington, which ultimately secured important civil rights legislation. Throughout his tenure as a civil rights activist, Rustin remained a committed pacifist and championed human rights not only at home but on an international level as well. Rustin—a gay man—also included in his civil rights agenda efforts to end bigotry and violence against lesbian and gay Americans. He continued to support minority rights until his death in 1987.

Mary Church Terrell

Mary Church Terrell was born to former slaves in Memphis, Tennessee, in 1863. Her father, Robert Church, was a pioneer businessman and landowner and eventually became the city's first black millionaire. Although Terrell's parents divorced when she was three years old, Robert Church continued to ensure that his daughter lived a life of privilege and education.

In 1884 Terrell became one of the first black women to complete college. At the same time that she launched a teaching career, she earned a graduate degree from Oberlin College in 1888. Upon graduation, Terrell embarked on a "grand tour," a two-year educational excursion through Europe during which she became fluent in French, German, and Italian.

Two events profoundly affected Terrell's life in the early 1890s. The first and happier event was her marriage to Robert Terrell, a Harvard magna cum laude graduate and Howard University law school valedictorian. The second, and more unsettling event was the lynching of her childhood friend Thomas Moss. Deeply moved by this experience, Terrell dedicated the next forty years of her life to social activism, speaking out for women's suffrage and against Jim Crow segregation laws. She became nationally known when she published her poignant autobiography, *A Colored Woman in a White World*. Terrell died in 1954 at the age of ninety, just months after a Supreme Court decision ended school segregation.

George Wallace

Born in 1919, George Wallace was raised in Alabama, where his father was a farmer. He attended the University of Alabama, graduating in 1942 with a law degree.

During World War II, Wallace served on a bomber squad in the U.S. Air Force, participating in a number of bombing campaigns in the Pacific. Shortly after the war, Wallace entered politics, becoming the assistant attorney general for Alabama governor Chauncey Sparks. He served in the Alabama state legislature from 1947 until 1952, when he became a district court judge. Outspoken, bellicose, and openly critical of the federal government, Wallace earned the nickname "the Fighting Little Judge." He stood out, too, for his defiant stance against integration.

After an unsuccessful gubernatorial race in 1958, Wallace—by a landslide vote—was elected governor of Alabama in 1962. In his inaugural address, he vowed to resist court-ordered integration in the schools; a year later, he personally blocked two black students from enrolling at the University of Alabama, capitulating only when President John F. Kennedy federalized the national guard.

He was reelected governor in 1970 and again in 1974. During a string of unsuccessful bids for the U.S. presidency, Wallace was shot and paralyzed while campaigning in a shopping mall in 1972. After attempting to reconcile with African Americans and recanting his white supremacist positions, he was elected governor of Alabama again in 1982. He retired from public life in 1987, remaining in Montgomery until his death in 1998.

Booker T. Washington

Booker Taliaferro Washington was born into slavery on a plantation near Hales Ford, Virginia, sometime around 1858. He lived in squalor, his broken-down, dirt-floor cabin doubling as the open-fire kitchen for his mother, the plantation's cook. He never knew his father, rumored to be a white man from a nearby plantation. When the Civil War ended in 1865, Washington's young family walked several hundred miles to the salt mines just outside of Charleston, West Virginia. Although only a small child, Washington began working in the salt furnaces, where he spent long hours packing salt barrels. After years of this backbreaking work, the teenage Washington was forced to descend into the coal mines, a dark and dangerous job that he dreaded. It was deep in these mines that Washington first overheard two workers talking about Hampton, a school for any race, open to those willing to work for their board and tuition. Washington would later describe this turning point in his autobiography:

> As they went on describing the school, it seemed to me that it must be the greatest place on earth, and not even Heaven presented more attractions for me at that time than did the Hampton Normal and Agricultural Institute in Virginia, about which these men were talking. I resolved at once to go to that school. . . . I remembered only that I was on fire constantly with one ambition, and that was to go to Hampton.

When he turned sixteen, Washington made the arduous five-hundred-mile trek to Hampton, arriving hungry and nearly penniless. He secured a position as janitor and threw himself into his studies. It was during his three years there that Washington adopted the belief that through vocational education—the acquisition of real, practical trade skills—the black race could become a contributing segment of society. Eventually, Washington became a teacher at Hampton, and from there he helped found a vocational school, the Tuskegee Normal and Industrial Institute, in Alabama in 1881. He was approximately twenty-three years old.

Over the next twenty years, Washington built Tuskegee into the largest black institution in America. As he taught, he continued to exhort blacks to better themselves. His lifelong philosophy that accommodation and education would lead to black advancement won Washington overwhelming support from white society. At the same time, many black leaders, most notably W.E.B. Du Bois, criticized this approach to race relations, claiming that it stunted black intellectual growth.

Washington spent the rest of his life as an educator, writer, and speaker. He died at Tuskegee in 1915.

Roy Wilkins

Roy Wilkins was born in 1901. He was raised by his aunt and uncle in St. Paul, Minnesota, and although poor, Wilkins worked hard and excelled in the integrated public school that he attended as a child. While attending the University of Minnesota, Wilkins joined the National Association for the Advancement of Colored People (NAACP). In addition to his growing civil rights activism, Wilkins served as an editor for both the school paper and a weekly, the *St. Paul Appeal*. Graduating with a bachelor's degree in sociology in 1923, Wilkins, an accomplished writer and editor by this time, took a job at another black weekly, the *Kansas City Call*, where he would remain for the next eight years.

An articulate speaker and effective organizer, Wilkins was appointed assistant executive secretary of the NAACP in 1931. Three years later, Wilkins succeeded W.E.B. Du Bois as editor of *Crisis*, the organization's official magazine. At the same time, he organized and led numerous events to promote black rights, including the National Emergency Civil Rights Mobilization, an organization that promoted fair employment practices.

In 1955 Wilkins became executive secretary of the NAACP, a position he would hold for twenty-two years. In that capacity, Wilkins worked tirelessly to dismantle the forces that kept blacks mired in poverty and second-class citizenship. An eloquent speaker and writer, Wilkins addressed a wide array of audiences—including congressmen and presidents—and wrote extensively in all types of publications to spread the message of the NAACP. For a brief period in the late 1960s and early 1970s, Wilkins came under attack from more militant blacks, who rejected the nonviolent philosophy that Wilkins embraced. He retired from the NAACP in 1977 and died four years later.

Whitney M. Young Jr.

Whitney M. Young Jr. is most often remembered as a strong force in the Urban League—and as a tireless advocate for black rights in general. Born in Kentucky in 1921, Young attended Kentucky State College. Then, during World War II, Young served in an antiaircraft company that, although made up primarily of African American soldiers, was directed by white officers—a degrading experience that spurred Young's interest in civil rights issues.

After the war, Young attended the University of Minnesota, where he earned a graduate degree in social work in 1947. A charismatic and eloquent speaker, Young continued his career in academia as a university lecturer. In 1954 he was named dean of the School of Social Work at Atlanta University.

In 1960 Young was appointed executive director of the Urban League. In this role, Young not only created thousands of jobs for black Americans, but he also brought a host of civil rights issues to the forefront of the American consciousness. In his quest to boost black participation in society, Young frequently testified before Congress and often spoke to business and civic leaders to promote black leadership and equal economic opportunity. He served on a number of presidential committees during the Kennedy and Johnson administrations, including Youth Employment and the National Advisory Council on Economic Progress. Also noteworthy, Young played a key role in launching the historic 1963 March on Washington.

In 1971 Young's life was cut tragically short when he drowned while swimming in Lagos, Nigeria, where he was attending a conference that centered on race relations. He was fifty-one years old. Today, the Urban League continues to host its annual fund-raising event, the Whitney M. Young Jr. Award Dinner. Started in 1974, the event attracts a wide range of political leaders and celebrities, draws national media coverage, and raises more than $1 million a year.

Chronology

1619
The first African slaves are brought to North America.

1863
President Abraham Lincoln issues the Emancipation Proclamation.

1865
The Reconstruction era begins; the Thirteenth Amendment abolishes slavery in the United States.

1866
The Civil Rights Act of 1866 grants blacks U.S. citizenship; the Fourteenth Amendment reaffirms citizenship rights for blacks and gives all citizens full and equal protection under the law.

1870
The Fifteenth Amendment grants black males the right to vote.

1875
The Civil Rights Act of 1875 guarantees black Americans equal access to public facilities.

1876
Reconstruction ends.

1881
Booker T. Washington founds the Tuskegee Institute, a vocational school for blacks.

1883
The Supreme Court overturns the Civil Rights Act of 1875.

1890
The state of Mississippi adopts poll taxes and literacy tests to disenfranchise black voters.

1895
Booker T. Washington delivers his Atlanta Exposition speech, which accepts segregation of the races.

1896
The Supreme Court rules in *Plessy v. Ferguson* that separate but equal treatment of the races is constitutional.

1900–1915
Over one thousand blacks are lynched in the states of the former Confederacy.

1905
The Niagara Movement is founded by W.E.B. Du Bois and other black leaders to urge more direct action to achieve black civil rights.

1909
The National Association for the Advancement of Colored People (NAACP) is organized.

1910
The National Urban League is founded to help the conditions of urban African Americans.

1925
Black nationalist leader Marcus Garvey is convicted of mail fraud.

1928
For the first time in the twentieth century an African American is elected to Congress.

1931
Farrad Muhammad establishes in Detroit what will become the Black Muslim Movement.

1933
The NAACP files—and loses—its first suit against segregation and discrimination in education.

1938
The Supreme Court orders the admission of a black applicant to the University of Missouri Law School.

1941
A. Philip Randolph threatens a massive march on Washington unless the Roosevelt administration takes measures to ensure black employment in defense industries; Roosevelt agrees to establish the Fair Employment Practices Committee (FEPC).

1942
The Congress of Racial Equality (CORE) is organized in Chicago.

1943
Race riots in Detroit and Harlem cause black leaders to ask their followers to be less demanding in asserting their commitment to civil rights; A. Philip Randolph breaks ranks to call for civil disobedience against Jim Crow schools and railroads.

1946
The Supreme Court, in *Morgan v. The Commonwealth of Virginia*, rules that state laws requiring racial segregation on buses violate the Constitution when applied to interstate passengers.

April 1947
Jackie Robinson breaks the color line in major league baseball.

April 9–23, 1947
Bayard Rustin organizes integrated group trips on trains and buses through Kentucky, Tennessee, North Carolina, and Virginia.

October 29, 1947
To Secure These Rights, the report by the President's Committee on Civil Rights, is released; the commission, appointed by President Harry S. Truman, calls for the elimination of racial segregation and recommends government action to secure civil rights for all Americans.

July 26, 1948
President Harry S. Truman issues an executive order desegregating the armed services.

June 1950
The NAACP decides to make its legal strategy a full-scale attack on educational segregation.

May 17, 1954
In *Brown v. Board of Education* the Supreme Court declares separate educational facilities "inherently unequal."

July 11, 1954
The First White Citizens Council meeting is held in Mississippi.

September 1954
The school year begins with the integration of 150 formerly segregated school districts in eight states; many other school districts remain segregated.

May 31, 1955
The Supreme Court, rejecting the NAACP's plea for complete and total desegregation by September 1955, orders desegregation "with all deliberate speed."

September 23, 1955
An all-white jury finds defendants innocent of murdering black teenager Emmett Till after a nationally publicized trial; the defendants later confess to the killing.

November 1955
The Interstate Commerce Commission (ICC) bans racial seg-

regation in all facilities and vehicles engaged in interstate transportation.

December 1, 1955
Rosa Parks is arrested for refusing to give up her bus seat to a white person; the action triggers a bus boycott in Montgomery, Alabama, led by Martin Luther King Jr.

January 30, 1956
The home of Martin Luther King Jr. is bombed.

February 3, 1956
Autherine Lucy wins a federal court order admitting her to the University of Alabama only to have the university permanently "expel" her; the University of Alabama remains segregated for seven more years.

March 12, 1956
One hundred one members of Congress from the South sign the "Southern Manifesto," decrying the *Brown v. Board of Education* decision.

June 1, 1956
Alabama outlaws the NAACP.

December 21, 1956
The Montgomery bus boycott ends after the city receives U.S. Supreme Court order to desegregate city buses.

January 11, 1957
Martin Luther King Jr. and a number of Southern black clergymen create the Southern Christian Leadership Conference (SCLC).

August 29, 1957
Congress passes the first civil rights legislation since Reconstruction: The Civil Rights Act of 1957 establishes a civil rights division at the Justice Department and provides penalties for violating the voting rights of a U.S. citizen.

September 4, 1957
On the orders of Arkansas governor Orval Faubus, Arkansas National Guardsmen block nine black students from entering Central High School in Little Rock.

September 24, 1957
President Dwight D. Eisenhower dispatches one thousand paratroopers of the 101st Airborne Division to Little Rock to enforce a federal court order integrating Central High School.

September 29, 1958
The Supreme Court, in *Cooper v. Aaron*, rules that "evasive schemes" cannot be used to circumvent school desegregation.

October 25, 1958
Ten thousand students hold a Youth March for Integrated Schools in Washington, D.C.

1959
Sit-in campaigns by college students desegregate eating facilities in St. Louis, Chicago, and Bloomington, Indiana; the Tennessee Christian Leadership Conference holds brief sit-ins in Nashville department stores.

February 1, 1960
Four black students stage a sit-in at a Woolworth's lunch counter in Greensboro, North Carolina; the sit-in movement to desegregate Southern restaurants, hotels, movie theaters, libraries, and parks spreads to other Southern states.

April 1960
The Student Nonviolent Coordinating Committee (SNCC) is formed at a student conference in Raleigh, North Carolina.

April 19, 1960
Twenty-five hundred students and community members in Nashville, Tennessee, stage a march on city hall—the first major demonstration of the civil rights movement—following the bombing of the home of a black lawyer.

May 6, 1960
President Eisenhower signs civil rights legislation authorizing federal judges to appoint referees to assist blacks seeking to register and to vote.

June 30, 1960
Zaire becomes the first of eleven African countries to gain independence within one year, inspiring many American blacks.

October 19, 1960
Martin Luther King Jr. is arrested during an Atlanta sit-in; Democratic presidential candidate John F. Kennedy telephones Mrs. King to express concern.

November 8, 1960
John F. Kennedy is elected president by a narrow margin.

December 5, 1960
The Supreme Court rules that discrimination in bus terminal restaurants is a violation of the Interstate Commerce Act.

March 13, 1961
James Farmer, national director of CORE, calls for volunteers to conduct "Freedom Rides" throughout the South.

Spring 1961
Martin Luther King Jr. and President John F. Kennedy hold a secret meeting at which King learns that the new president will not push hard for new civil rights legislation.

May 1961
White and black Freedom Riders are arrested and assaulted in North and South Carolina and Alabama; one bus is burned by a white mob. The CORE-sponsored Freedom Ride disbands and the movement is taken over by SNCC volunteers; the Kennedy administration sends federal marshals to assure the safety of the Freedom Riders.

June 16, 1961
U.S. attorney general Robert Kennedy meets with civil rights leaders and urges them to forgo demonstrations and Freedom Rides and to concentrate on winning the right to vote.

November 1961
Local black organizations in Albany, Georgia, form the Albany Movement to demonstrate for voting rights and desegregation.

December 1961
The SCLC meets with AFL-CIO leaders to strengthen ties between the two organizations.

December 11–14, 1961
Hundreds of demonstrators participate in marches in Albany, Georgia. Martin Luther King Jr. and aides arrive on December 15.

January 1962
FBI director J. Edgar Hoover writes Attorney General Robert Kennedy concerning Martin Luther King Jr.'s alleged ties to the Communist Party.

May 31, 1962
James Meredith files suit claiming racial discrimination after he is denied admission to the University of Mississippi.

August 1962
Albany Movement ends with many of its goals unmet.

August 7, 1962
A SNCC Voter Registration School opens in Pike County, Mississippi, marking the first such effort in the history of the state.

September 1962
Ku Klux Klan dynamite blasts destroy four black churches in Georgia towns.

September 30, 1962
President Kennedy federalizes the national guard and sends several hundred federal marshals to Mississippi to guarantee James Meredith's admission to the University of Mississippi Law School over the opposition of Governor Ross Barnett and other whites; two persons are killed in a campus riot.

November 20, 1962
President Kennedy signs an executive order barring racial discrimination in federally financed housing.

February 2, 1963
Martin Luther King Jr. and other SCLC leaders arrive in Birmingham, Alabama, to lead a civil rights campaign; Robert Kennedy labels the effort "ill-timed" and urges King to abandon it.

Spring 1963
CORE takes the lead in protesting discrimination in Northern cities.

April 1963
Martin Luther King Jr. opens his campaign to desegregate Birmingham and is arrested on April 12; while incarcerated, King composes his "Letter from Birmingham City Jail."

May 3, 1963
Birmingham police chief Eugene "Bull" Connor turns police dogs and fire hoses against nonviolent demonstrators in Birmingham.

May 5, 1963
Three thousand protesters are jailed in Birmingham—the largest number of people imprisoned at any one time in the history of the civil rights movement.

May 10, 1963
An accord is reached in Birmingham; within ninety days lunch counters, rest rooms, and drinking fountains will be desegregated in the city.

June 11, 1963
Black students Vivian Malone and James Hood enter the University of Alabama despite a demonstration of resistance by Governor George Wallace; in a nationally televised speech President John F. Kennedy calls segregation morally wrong.

June 12, 1963
NAACP field secretary Medgar Evers is shot and killed as he enters his home in Jackson, Mississippi.

June 19, 1963
Leaders of nearly one hundred corporations meet in New York City to pledge financial support for the civil rights movement.

July 18–23, 1963
Riots in Harlem follow the shooting of a fifteen-year-old black youth by an off-duty police officer.

August 28, 1963
Over 250,000 Americans gather at the Lincoln Memorial to urge the passage of civil rights legislation and hear Martin Luther King Jr. deliver his "I Have a Dream" speech. Malcolm X dismisses the march as "the Farce on Washington."

September 15, 1963
Four young girls are killed when a bomb explodes at a Baptist church in Birmingham, Alabama.

October 10, 1963
Attorney General Robert Kennedy authorizes the wiretapping of Martin Luther King Jr.'s home phone in Atlanta.

November 22, 1963
President John F. Kennedy is assassinated; Vice President Lyndon B. Johnson assumes the presidency.

January 8, 1964
President Lyndon B. Johnson calls for passage of a civil rights act in his State of the Union address.

April 26, 1964
SNCC workers organize the Mississippi Freedom Democratic Party (MFDP).

Summer 1964
Enlisting the help of white volunteers, SNCC and CORE seek to register black voters across the South in the "Freedom Summer" campaign.

June 21, 1964
Three civil rights workers, Michael Schwerner and Andrew Goodman, both white New Yorkers, and James Chaney, a black student from Meridian, Mississippi, are murdered near Philadelphia, Mississippi.

July 2, 1964
President Lyndon B. Johnson signs the Civil Rights Act of 1964, which prohibits discrimination in most public accommodations, authorizes the federal government to withhold funds from programs practicing discrimination, and creates the Equal Employment Opportunity Commission.

July 29, 1964
Several national civil rights leaders call for a moratorium on mass marches and demonstrations until after the November 3 presidential election.

August 22–26, 1964
At the Democratic National Convention in Atlantic City, New Jersey, delegates of the Mississippi Freedom Democratic Party ask to be seated as the legitimate Democratic Party of Mississippi; they refuse the compromise offer of two delegate seats.

September 14, 1964
New York City begins a program to end segregation by busing students.

November 3, 1964
Lyndon B. Johnson, with heavy black support, wins the presidential election by a wide margin over Barry Goldwater.

December 10, 1964
Martin Luther King Jr. is awarded the Nobel Peace Prize.

February 18, 1965
Civil rights marcher Jimmie Lee Jackson is shot and killed in Marion, Alabama.

February 21, 1965
Malcolm X is assassinated while addressing a rally of his followers in New York City; three black men are ultimately convicted of the murder.

March 7, 1965
"Bloody Sunday": Six hundred marchers outside Selma, Alabama, are attacked by state troopers with nightsticks and tear gas.

March 9, 1965
Martin Luther King Jr. leads a voting rights march in Selma but turns back before a state trooper barricade.

March 11, 1965
The death of white Unitarian minister James J. Reeb following a beating by local whites in Selma triggers demonstrations in many Northern cities.

March 15, 1965
President Johnson delivers a televised speech to a joint session of Congress to request passage of a voting rights act.

March 21–25, 1965
Following a federal judge's court order allowing the march, and under federalized protection, Martin Luther King Jr. leads a voting rights march from Selma to Montgomery, Alabama.

August 6, 1965
President Johnson signs the Voting Rights Act of 1965, which outlaws literacy tests and empowers the Justice Department to supervise federal elections in seven Southern states.

August 11–16, 1965
Rioting in the black ghetto of Watts in Los Angeles leads to thirty-five deaths, nine hundred injuries, and over thirty-five hundred arrests.

January 1966
Martin Luther King Jr. moves to Chicago to begin his first civil rights campaign in a northern city.

March 25, 1966
The Supreme Court bans poll taxes for all elections.

May 16, 1966
Stokely Carmichael replaces John Lewis as chairman of SNCC.

June 6, 1966
James Meredith is shot by a sniper while on a one-man "march against fear" in Mississippi.

June 7–26, 1966
Other civil rights leaders, including King and Carmichael, complete the "Meredith march"; the slogan "black power" is first used by Carmichael.

July 1966
The CORE national convention adopts a resolution in support of black power; the NAACP convention officially opposes the doctrine.

August 5, 1966
Martin Luther King Jr. leads an integrated march in Chicago and is wounded when whites throw bottles and bricks at demonstrators.

October 1966
The Black Panther Party (BPP) is founded in Oakland, California.

December 1966
SNCC votes to exclude whites from membership.

February 25, 1967
Martin Luther King Jr. delivers his first speech devoted entirely to the war in Vietnam, which he calls "one of history's most cruel and senseless wars"; his position causes estrangement with President Johnson and is criticized by the NAACP.

May 4, 1967
Alabama sheriffs James Clark and Al Lingo are among those who fail to get renominated in Democratic primaries that have significant black participation.

May 10–11, 1967
Rioting at all-black Jackson State College in Mississippi leads to one death and two serious injuries.

June 13, 1967
Thurgood Marshall is the first black to be nominated to serve on the Supreme Court.

June 19, 1967
A federal judge orders Washington, D.C., schools to end de facto school segregation.

July 1967
Rioting in the black ghetto of Newark, New Jersey, leaves 23 dead and 725 injured; rioting in Detroit leave 43 dead and 324 injured; President Johnson appoints Governor Otto Kerner of Illinois to head a commission to investigate recent urban riots.

February 29, 1968
The Kerner Commission issues its report, warning that the nation is "moving toward two societies, one black, one white—separate and unequal."

March 18, 1968
Martin Luther King Jr. travels to Memphis, Tennessee, to help settle a garbage workers' strike.

April 4, 1968
Martin Luther King Jr. is assassinated by James Earl Ray in Memphis, Tennessee, precipitating riots in more than one hundred cities.

April 11, 1968
Congress passes civil rights legislation prohibiting racial discrimination in the sale or rental of housing.

May 11, 1968
Ralph Abernathy, Martin Luther King Jr.'s successor as head of the SCLC, leads Poor People's Campaign in Washington, D.C.

October 30, 1969
The Supreme Court replaces its 1954 decision calling for "all deliberate speed" in school desegregation by unanimously ordering that all segregation in schools must end "at once."

1971
The Supreme Court grants federal courts the authority to order busing to desegregate public schools.

1984
Jesse Jackson launches a campaign for the U.S. presidency.

1992
Riots break out in South Central Los Angeles after an all-white jury acquits four white police officers who were videotaped beating African American motorist Rodney King.

1995
Legions of black Americans gather in Washington, D.C., to participate in the Million Man March.

For Further Research

RALPH ABERNATHY, *And the Walls Came Tumbling Down.* New York: Harper & Row, 1989.

JERVIS ANDERSON, *Bayard Rustin: Troubles I've Seen: A Biography.* San Francisco: HarperCollins, 1997.

HARRY S. ASHMORE, *Civil Rights and Wrongs: A Memoir of Race and Politics.* New York: Pantheon, 1994.

NUMAN V. BARTLEY, *The Rise of Massive Resistance.* Baton Rouge: Louisiana State University Press, 1969.

SALLY BELFRAGE, *Freedom Summer.* New York: Viking, 1965.

TAYLOR BRANCH, *Parting the Waters: America in the King Years, 1954–1963.* New York: Simon & Schuster, 1988.

GEORGE BREITMAN, *The Last Years of Malcolm X.* New York: Pathfinder, 1970.

STOKELY CARMICHAEL AND CHARLES V. HAMILTON, *Black Power: The Politics of Liberation in America.* New York: Vintage Books, 1967.

CLAYBORNE CARSON, ED., *The Movement: 1964–1970.* New York: Greenwood, 1993.

W.S. CASH, *The Mind of the South.* New York: Knopf, 1941.

E. CULPEPPER CLARK, *The Schoolhouse Door: Segregation's Last Stand at the University of Alabama.* New York: Oxford University Press, 1993.

E. DAVID CRONON, *Black Moses.* Madison: University of Wisconsin Press, 1968.

DANIEL S. DAVIS, *Mr. Black Labor: The Story of A. Philip Randolph, Father of the Civil Rights Movement.* New York: E.P. Dutton, 1972.

TOWNSEND DAVIS, *Weary Feet, Rested Souls: A Guided His-*

tory Through the Civil Rights Movement. New York: W.W. Norton, 1998.

W.E.B. DU BOIS, *The Souls of Black Folk*. New York: Dodd, Mead, 1979.

CHARLES EVERS, *Have No Fear: The Charles Evers Story*. New York: John Wiley & Sons, 1996.

JAMES FARMER, *Lay Bare the Heart: An Autobiography of the Civil Rights Movement*. New York: Arbor House, 1985.

JOHN HOPE FRANKLIN AND ALFRED A. MOSS JR., *From Slavery to Freedom: A History of African Americans*. New York: McGraw Hill, 1994.

LORRAINE HANSBERRY, *The Movement: Documentary of a Struggle for Equality*. New York: Simon & Schuster, 1964.

JAMES HASKINS, *The Life and Death of Martin Luther King Jr.* New York: Lothrop, Lee, and Shephard, 1977.

LANGSTON HUGHES, *Fight for Freedom: The Story of the NAACP*. New York: W.W. Norton, 1962.

MARTIN LUTHER KING JR., *Stride Toward Freedom: The Montgomery Story*. New York: Harper & Row, 1958.

———, *Why We Can't Wait*. New York: Harper & Row, 1963.

RICHARD KLUGER, *Simple Justice*. New York: Knopf, 1975.

PETER B. LEVY, ED., *Let Freedom Ring: A Documentary History of the Civil Rights Movement*. New York: Praeger, 1992.

HOWARD LINDSEY, *A History of Black America*. Secaucus, NJ: Chartwell Books, 1994.

MALCOLM X, WITH ALEX HALEY, *The Autobiography of Malcolm X*. New York: Grove, 1965.

THURGOOD MARSHALL, *Dream Makers, Dream Breakers: The World of Justice*. Boston: Little, Brown, 1993.

Doug McAdam, *Freedom Summer.* New York: Oxford University Press, 1988.

August Meier and Elliott Rudwick, *CORE: A Study in the Civil Rights Movement, 1942–1968.* New York: Oxford University Press, 1973.

Kay Mills, *This Little Light of Mine: The Life of Fannie Lou Hamer.* New York: Penguin, 1992.

Benjamin Muse, *The American Negro Revolution: From Nonviolence to Black Power, 1960–1961.* Bloomington: Indiana University Press, 1973.

Victor Navasky, *Kennedy Justice.* New York: Atheneum, 1971.

Stephen B. Oates, *Let the Trumpet Sound: A Life of Martin Luther King Jr.* New York: HarperPerennial, 1994.

Martin Oppenheimer, *The Sit-In Movement of 1960.* Brooklyn, NY: Carlson, 1989.

Fred Powledge, *Free at Last? The Civil Rights Movement and the People Who Made It.* Boston: Little, Brown, 1991.

Howell Raines, ed., *My Soul Is Rested: Movement Days in the Deep South Remembered.* New York: Penguin, 1983.

Cedric Robinson, *Black Movements in America.* New York: Routledge, 1997.

Bayard Rustin, *Down the Line.* Chicago: Quadrangle, 1971.

Eric J. Sundquist, ed., *Frederick Douglass: New Literary and Historical Essays.* New York: Cambridge University Press, 1990.

Herman E. Talmadge, *You and Segregation.* Birmingham, AL: Vulcan, 1955.

James M. Washington, ed., *A Testament of Hope.* San Francisco: Harper & Row, 1986.

ROBERT WEISBROT, *Freedom Bound*. New York: W.W. Norton, 1990.

NANCY J. WEISS, *Whitney M. Young and the Struggle for Civil Rights*. Princeton, NJ: Princeton University Press, 1989.

ROY WILKINS, *Talking It Over with Roy Wilkins: Selected Speeches and Writings*. Norwalk, CT: M&B, 1977.

BRENDA WILKINSON, *Jesse Jackson: Still Fighting for the Dream*. Englewood Cliffs, NJ: Silver Burdett, 1990.

JUAN WILLIAMS, *Eyes on the Prize: America's Civil Rights Years, 1954–1965*. New York: Viking, 1987.

ANDREW J. YOUNG, *An Easy Burden: The Civil Rights Movement and the Transformation of America*. San Francisco: HarperCollins, 1996.

WHITNEY M. YOUNG JR., *Beyond Racism: Building an Open Society*. New York: McGraw Hill, 1969.

HOWARD ZINN, *The New Abolitionists*. Boston: Beacon, 1964.

Index

affirmative action, 178
African Americans
  average income of, 77
  becoming familiar with statutes
    protecting rights of, 110–13
  broken promises to, 78–79
  cause for optimism by, 177–78
  civil war between whites and, 54
  creating employment opportunities
    for, 96–98
  cultivating friendly relations with
    whites, 32–33
  denial of capital to, 190–92, 193,
    194
  dignity of, 83–84
  economic disparity between whites
    and, 26
  efforts for growth and progress by,
    34–35
  first, elected to Congress, 215
  goal of equality for, 103–104
  home purchases by, 193–94
  hope and encouragement of, 35–36
  injustices and inequalities of, 59–60
  leadership from, 94–96
  Martin Luther King's advice to,
    60–61
  Martin Luther King's dream for,
    62–63
  need for organization by, 107–108
  potential influence of individual,
    187–88
  pressure on, to achieve in university
    studies, 182–85
  progress made by, 178–79, 188–89
    as not meaningful, 75–77
  property ownership by, 192–93
  quest for identity by, 79–80
  self-sufficiency by, 104–107
  stereotyping of, 179–82
  supporting leadership of, 98–99
  tensions between Jews and, 155–56
  as trapped in a vicious cycle, 51
  unemployment and, 85, 130, 178
  vs. voluntary immigrants, 91–92
  whites cultivating friendly relations

  with, 33–34
  working within political institutions,
    149–50
  see also discrimination and prejudice;
    integration; separatism
Albany Movement, 18–19, 221
antiracist racism, 150
anti-Semitism, 105
apartheid, 160–63
Arab Americans, 156
Asian Americans, 156
Atlanta Exposition, 32–36, 215

Barnett, Ross, 19
Biddle, Francis, 113
Birmingham, Alabama, 223
Black Panther Party, 22, 227
Black Power, 226
  African American criticism of,
    127–28
  vs. integration, 147–48
  meaning of, 93–94
  overtones and implications of, 93
  SNCC and, 22
  white people on, 150–51
  without becoming chauvinistic,
    80–81
  see also separatism
blacks. See African Americans
Bloody Sunday, 20–21, 225
boycotts, 16–17, 218
Brown, John, 40
Brown v. Board of Education of
  Topeka, Kansas (1954), 15, 217, 218

Cantarella, Marcia, 177, 196
Carmichael, Stokely, 144, 196–97, 226
Chaney, James, 224
church, bombing of, 223
civil rights
  defined, 109–10
  John F. Kennedy on, 119–21
  Lyndon B. Johnson on, 138–43
  as a moral issue, 121
Civil Rights Act
  of 1866, 13, 111, 215

233